CLOCKS AND WHISTLES

A Play by

SAMUEL
ADAMSON

AMBER LANE PRESS

First published in 1996 by
Amber Lane Press Ltd,
Cheorl House, Church Street, Charlbury, Oxford OX7 3PR
Telephone and fax: 01608 810024

Printed in Great Britain
by The Guernsey Press Company, C.I.

ISBN 1 872868 16 9

CHARACTERS

Henry — 25
Anne — 26
Trevor — 25
Alec — late 40s/early 50s
Caroline — late 30s

London, The Present

Clocks and Whistles was first presented at the Bush Theatre, London, on 2nd April 1996, with the following cast:

Henry ... John Light

Anne ... Kate Beckinsale

Trevor ... Neil Stuke

Alec ... Michael Cashman

Caroline ... Melanie Thaw

Directed by Dominic Dromgoole

Designed by Paul Andrews

Lighting by Paul Russell

Scene 1

A pub, SW3. **Henry** *and* **Anne** *are sitting at a table. Soft music.* **Henry** *is writing in his diary.* **Anne** *has been drinking, but is in control. Long pause.* **Anne** *raps her fingers on the table. She sighs. Pause.*

Anne Alec is due at my place this afternoon. (*Beat.*) He might take me to a film. (*Beat.*) Well, I know what you think of Alec. (*Beat.*) Frappy?

Henry I don't think anything about Alec.

Anne I don't like him much, either.

    (*Beat.*)

Henry (*head down, writing*) I know too little about him to have an opinion either way. As you know.

Anne Do you know what I hate? I hate supermodels, minor royalty and finely featured English actresses with dead — or alive — French husbands ...

Henry (*not looking up*) Do you want another one?

Anne (*fed up*) Do I? No, no more.

Henry OK.

Anne This is very rude.

Henry What?

Anne Writing in your diary, while you're with me. I'm bored.

Henry Have another drink. I won't be long — you've never minded before.

Anne What does it say?

Henry Stuff.

Anne That's not an answer. Stuff. Have you written things in there about Alec? I bet you have. You hate Alec.

Henry Tell me about him.

    (*Pause.* **Anne** *doesn't answer.*)

(*patiently*) No, I don't. Hate him.

(*Beat.*)

Anne Have you noticed my hair today? (*curls her fringe*) It stinks ... I mean, it doesn't smell, but it ... (*pats it down*) ... won't ... sit.

Henry What?

Anne This hair ... my bangs.

Henry (*still writing*) Love that word, bangs.

Anne This is a bad hair day, this one. I feel like ... (*makes a face*) I could turn people into stone. Here, touch it ... It's a damn mess.

Henry It looks fine to me, Anne.

(*Beat.*)

Anne What does it say, there? (*Pause.*) I shouldn't let you do this. I should be the one writing in my diary, being all creative, showing off in public, while *you* sit staring into thin air. (*Pause.*) Heigh, ho.

Henry (*busy*) I'm not ... showing off ...

Anne Go back a few pages.

Henry No.

Anne Go on, go back, tell me what's written on ... March 4th ...

Henry No.

Anne Pleeeaassee.

Henry (*flicks back a few pages*) "Meet Anne ... lunch. Palaminos." Happy? That's you. You're in it.

Anne I know it's not an appointments diary.

Henry It's that too.

Anne I'm not going there any more, it's revolting. I said to you, cannelloni has meat in it, you said, "Um, I don't know ... I think cannelloni has whatever you want to put in it, it doesn't have to be meat. What's it say on the menu?" We look at the menu and it just says "Cannelloni". (*Pause.*) Cannelloni *has* meat in it, Frappy. I've never, *ever* known cannelloni not

8

not to have meat in it. And there was gelatine in my pudding. I'm not going there any more.

Henry All right. That's fine with me.

Anne The waiters aren't what they were, anyway.

Henry No, they're not ...

Anne Very nice once, I remember.

Henry Me too.

(*Beat*.)

Anne There was a film on last night with a friend of mine in it, did you see it? She was *ghastly*.

Henry I watched an interview. Helen Mirren.

Anne Oh, now *she* is adorable. (*sighs*) What I wouldn't give. (*looking at the diary*) What's that, sticking out the back?

Henry It's a note from you.

Anne Let me see.

Henry No. (*Beat; reads*) "Dear Henry, we could get out of London altogether ..." (*turns the note*) "... although Fay Wray is on at the Everyman in Hampstead this evening. Love, Anne." There.

(*Pause*.)

Anne What?

(*Pause*.)

Henry Are you sure you don't want another one?

Anne I'll finish yours. (*takes his coffee*) Don't you like me any more, Henry?

Henry Of course ... what's the matter?

Anne Nothing, except you're not taking any notice of me. (*Pause*.) Here's to two-bit little south London theatres. (*drinks*) Urgh, it's cold.

(*Beat*.)

Henry It isn't two-bit.

Anne It *is*. (*Beat*.) The only thing I liked about that place was the smell.

9

Henry Smell?

Anne That incredible backstage smell. The floorboards ... old adrenalin. What does it say in your diary about it, bumping into me?

Henry I think I thought of Sibyl Vane.

Anne Who's that?

Henry *Dorian Gray.*

Anne Yes, right. You in a box watching me ...

Henry ... playing who? — Rosalind ... your white, soft skin, with flushes of pink on the cheekbones, glowing radiantly ...

Anne (*over this*) You're sweet, Frappy, but —

Henry (*continuing*) ... your pouting lips, your piercing eyes, your powerful, bony figure that spoke "ACTRESS", not like Sibyl Vane at all, more like a forties movie star. Hepburn in *Holiday*.

Anne (*depressed*) Oh, Hepburn ... why can't I be like her? Don't laugh.

> (*Beat.*)

Henry You'll get work.

Anne Guess what. I had an audition.

Henry Oh, Anne! You didn't tell me? Is it a film? What?

Anne A play. You won't believe it. *Who's Afraid of Virginia Woolf?*

Henry (*incredulous*) Really?

Anne Yes.

Henry Elizabeth Taylor?

Anne No, I went for Honey, you know, the other one, the wimp.

> (**Henry** *smiles. Beat.*)

That was made in the thirties.

Henry What?

Anne *Holiday.*

Henry Wasn't.

10

Anne Was.

Henry Wasn't.

Anne Fuck it. Should I have another drink?

Henry I really don't care now.

Anne I can't afford it today.

Henry Please. I offered anyway.

    (*Beat.*)

Anne I'm not besieging you, am I?

Henry No.

Anne It's just ... (*suspicious*) Who's new?

Henry No one.

Anne There is somebody, I can tell. That's why you're being so distant — I know you — sitting there with your diary, not even getting a drink, having a bloody cappuccino on a Saturday afternoon ...

Henry What's wrong with that ...?

Anne There is somebody.

Henry There's not.

Anne There is.

Henry No, there's not.

Anne Well, that's a shame.

Henry Oh, Anne.

    (*Beat.*)

Anne What about that primitive guy you were talking about? A few weeks ago you were talking about someone you met in a club. You said he was primitive. (*Beat.*) Do you want to know the painting I like most in the National Gallery?

Henry Um ... no.

Anne It's very pedestrian to people in the know, I bet.

Henry Probably. Come on ... have another drink ...

Anne The people who really know about *art*. But it's my favourite, favourite, favourite. (*Beat.*) "Ophelia Among the Flowers" ...

11

Henry I know that one ...

Anne It was ruined for me the other day when an American couple started looking at it though.

Henry Why?

Anne We shouldn't share our art with the Americans. Maybe there should be prescribed American days.

Henry Alec's American.

Anne He's not American really.

(*Beat.*)

Henry What?

Anne What?

Henry Alec's not American?

Anne He has the accent because he lived there. (*Pause.*) I'm hungry.

Henry They have nuts.

Anne Do they have ice-cream?

Henry No ... I don't think so.

Anne I'll have zabaglione!

Henry Zabaglione?

Anne Gelati, Frappy. Zabaglione gelati.

Henry There's none, Anne. They don't have it.

Anne Well they should.

(*Pause.*)

Henry I'm really surprised to hear that Alec isn't American.

(*Beat.*)

Anne My audition was a calamity. I was very bad. W.I. stuff, church hall.

Henry I bet it was fine.

Anne I was bad. Fine isn't good enough, anyway. Critics say that. "Helen-bloody-Mirren gave 'fine' support."

(*Pause.* **Henry** *starts writing again.*)

Oh, bloody hell, don't start writing again.

(**Henry** *looks up briefly, then continues writing.*)

Oh sod bucket pooh shit. I know you're seeing someone. I'll have another drink. Gin. Another gin.

(*Music. Crossfade.*)

Scene 2

Hyde Park. **Henry** *and* **Trevor** *are sitting on the ground.* **Trevor** *drinks from a large bottle of Coke.*

Trevor There's a piece of fluff, still stands down there ...

Henry I've seen her!

Trevor She's probably been there for five 'undred years — she's got worn-down stilettos and a tatty leather jacket ...

Henry That's it. I saw her the other day, she stands near a phone box ...

Trevor She needs 'er roots done.

Henry It's so blatant. She's not really, is she ...?

Trevor She is! She doesn't get anyone though, never.

Henry It's not surprising.

(*Beat.*)

Trevor Nah, not lookin' like that. She doesn't pull a thing these days ...

Henry What, have you tried, or something?

Trevor Yeah, right.

Henry No, of course not ... I didn't mean ...

Trevor You 'ave to go to other places for that sort of thing.

Henry I'm not ... Oh, do you?

Trevor She's cheap, what d'you reckon?

Henry I suppose she would be.

(*Beat.*)

Trevor Why were you around this area, then? (*Pause.*) You said you were 'ere the other day.

13

Henry I ... I had your address, and I ...

Trevor You chickened out.

(**Henry** *is silent.*)

Did you see me flat?

Henry No, I gave up.

Trevor Well, there's not much around here but me, all the trade's pretty straight ... you should have come over.

Henry I ... just wanted to see you.

Trevor (*smiles*) It's over there, five minute walk. All in good time. (*Pause.*) Where do you live, then?

Henry Clapham.

Trevor Hardly ever get down that way any more. Occasionally I do, quite recently in fact — there are a few places I go to sometimes. Two Brewers, know it?

Henry Yeah.

Trevor I suppose you've got a great place.

Henry Why do you suppose that?

Trevor I dunno, somethin' about you, your manner. I thought you probably lived in this really expensive 'ouse in Pimlico or somethin'.

Henry It's cheap, where I live.

Trevor No kiddin'?

Henry Really cheap.

Trevor Just like that prozzie.

Henry Cheaper, I'd say. We shouldn't talk about her like that.

Trevor Why not? She's a lost cause. (*eyes* **Henry** *up and down.*) Love that shirt you're wearing.

Henry Do you?

Trevor I couldn't see myself in it though.

Henry I could.

Trevor (*mischievous*) Aaaahh, nice one. (*Beat.*) D'you live with anyone?

14

Henry Yeah. Another guy. Martin.

Trevor Oh ... 'e's your significant partner, then.

Henry Significant other.

Trevor What?

Henry I think they say significant other.

Trevor Yeah, well, it's crap, i'n't it? (*Beat.*) Words, words, words, words.

>   (*Beat.*)

Henry He's not, anyway. His girlfriend spends most of her time there.

Trevor I hate that. That's why I live on me own.

Henry It's pretty dingy to be honest.

Trevor I wouldn't worry. You can find somewhere else.

>   (*Beat.*)

Henry Am I a disaster?

Trevor What?

Henry Nothing ... I ... just ...

Trevor You're the fucking Titanic, you are. (*laughs*) Look at you.

Henry I've got these ... venetian blinds ... (*Short pause.*) In my flat. (*Pause.*) You wouldn't believe them. (*Pause.*) They're *multi-coloured*. Red. Mauve. Pink. In the kitchen, loo and living-room. I have a friend, Anne, she was nearly sick when she saw them.

>   (*Short pause.* **Trevor** *looks at him, expecting more to the story.*)

You should see them. (*Pause.*) Anne's a bit of an upstart anyway. (*Short pause.*) What a dump!

Trevor That's from some movie.

Henry Yeah. Two movies.

>   (*Beat.*)

Trevor Elizabeth Taylor, right? Yeah, bloody Liz Taylor says it in somethin'.

(*Beat.* **Trevor** *drinks.*)

Henry Trevor?

Trevor Yeah?

Henry I was being a bit ... well, dishonest before, about that ... woman ... you know, because I didn't want to sound so surprised, or anything, because the other day I ...

Trevor What?

Henry I rang, um ... an escort agency ... isn't that sad?

Trevor No ... no, no.

Henry It is ...

Trevor No, but mate, there's no need to spend all that money, you know. No need to spend any money at all. I can't imagine you needing to call out, I 'ave to say, you *don't* need the practice ...

Henry Trevor.

Trevor Well ...

> (*He brings his fingers up to his lips and blows a kiss into the air. Beat.*)

Henry This woman arrives.

Trevor Woman?

Henry And we have a bit of a chat. She says hello, I say hello back. "This is nice, here," she says. "Hello," I say, gulping. "No, it's not," I say, "it's a dump." "Hi," she says. "Hi," I say. "That's nice," she says, looking at my poster of Julia McKenzie and Millicent Martin in *Side by Side by Sondheim*. It was awkward.

Trevor Sounds it.

Henry And I try to have sex with her, right, and she tries to have sex with me, but it doesn't work ...

Trevor Oh ...

Henry And she says "Bye" and I say "Bye" ... and that was a really, really, really, *really* stupid thing to do ...

Trevor No it wasn't, mate, I'd ...

Henry (*interrupting*) "Bye," I said, and she walked down the stairs and her skirt rode up her arse, you know, really, really corny, it was, it made me feel as if I was ...

Trevor (*over this*) Yeah, seen it.

Henry ... in a movie or something ... and that was, I'm not sure, eighty pounds down the drain, all on Barclaycard — (*ashamed*) Imagine Penelope's face ...

Trevor Who's Penelope?

Henry My mother.

Trevor You call her Penelope?

Henry That's her name. (*Pause.*) Stuff Penelope.

(*Beat.*)

Trevor Does she know about you?

Henry Who, Mum?

Trevor Yeah.

Henry She doesn't know anything. (*Pause. He sighs.*) Everything's so static, lumpish.

(*Long pause.* **Trevor** *smiles.*)

Trevor (*flirtatious*) I feel like dancing.

Henry It's a bit early, isn't it?

Trevor Never too early. I know a place. I'll show you the flat next time. (*Beat.*) Yeah, I wanna dance.

(*Pause. Music. Crossfade.*)

Scene 3

Anne's *flat, Chelsea.* **Henry** *and* **Alec** *are sitting. Uncomfortable pause.*

Henry So you're not American?

Alec Pardon me?

Henry Anne told me that you aren't — actually — American.

Alec She did?

(*Beat.*)

Henry She was quite drunk, I don't know whether maybe, she was ... So are you, or not?

Alec Actually, no I'm not.

Henry I never thought to ask, I always assumed you were. You just spent time there?

Alec You make it sound like a prison sentence, which it wasn't, the US is my home, spiritually, constitutionally, intellectually — my God, intellectually — and politically, even. Sure, I spent time there, late seventies, all of the eighties, ten years, more. And I go back all the time. You're in business, right, talking all day — it's a very verbal culture, more verbal than here, right, *much* more — so, you pick up the accent, you can't help it.

Henry Oh.

Alec (*blunt*) And, to be perfectly honest, I decided to retain it. Anything to keep others from the God-awful truth.

Henry Which is what?

Alec It's a great liability, Henry, if people know you were actually *born* on this dreary little island.

Henry Really?

Alec The only English who foreigners have any requirement for are either dead, or actors.

Henry Why did you come back, then?

Alec No choice. Anne. She needs me. (*Beat.*) Do you want a drink of some sort?

Henry (*uncomfortable*) Um, no thanks — I just called in, that's all.

Alec On your way somewhere?

Henry No.

Alec You're in Chelsea a lot?

Henry No.

Alec (*urging him to have a drink*) Go on. She might be a while — I suppose you know what she's like once she gets on that blower.

Henry All right ... a small one. Shall I ... tell her?

Alec I think I should know where they are, by now. (*gets up*) What do you want?

Henry Um, a beer will be fine.

Alec Well, we got only cool designer beers here, is that a sure thing with you?

Henry Sure. I mean ... OK.

> (**Alec** *hands* **Henry** *a beer and mixes himself a drink. He remains standing.*)

Alec I'm just here for the morning, Henry. I've got to go over some figures with Anne. She has an audition, did you know?

Henry Yes, she told me.

Alec It's damn good news: she's had no work for some time ...

Henry No.

Alec Not only that, though, no prospects of work either — she wasn't auditioning for anything.

Henry It's tough work.

Alec All work's tough. Tough is good. There was something wrong, right, it was laziness: pure, simple. She should be at two, three, four, five, six, seven auditions a week. She gets lazy. She never rings her agent. I got her that agent. Which is why I have to keep coming back to London, to get her moving.

> (*Beat.*)

Henry We all have our off periods, I suppose.

Alec No, Henry, not all of us. She was ... out of the right circles. (*smiles*)

Henry I see her a bit, I thought she was —

Alec (*interrupting*) You know it then, you know how lazy she was getting.

Henry She always seems on the go to me.

Alec Doing the wrong things. She wasn't looking for any work. Just relied on the hand-outs.

Henry Hand-outs?

(*Pause.*)

Alec That's what they are. I don't suppose she's told you that, though.

Henry Well, um — (*drinks his beer*)

Alec Just how close are you? (*doesn't wait for an answer*) I look after her financial interests, Henry, did you know that?

Henry Well, sort of, but ... I just assumed ...

Alec I've done it since her parents went AWOL.

Henry AWOL?

Alec Yes, Henry. I've always thought drinking too much then disappearing off the face of the earth is AWOL. That is not responsible. Behaviour. (*smiles*) If I was family, I'd be perturbed about that kind of unfaithfulness. But: I'm not family, so it makes no odds to me.

Henry But ... it was a car accident.

Alec I'd be careful about your use of the word "accident". But that's past history. (*charming, smiling*) She's known me all her life. It feels like I've known her all mine, too. She's stayed with me in New York many, many times. When she was younger. "Shazam, Anne!" I used to say when she walked in. (*Beat.*) The father was useless in business, useless; I was grateful to take over some very frayed reins, 'cause I got what he didn't ... (*taps his head*) ... nous ... (*smiles and pauses*) So, you see her a lot?

Henry She's a good friend.

Alec Yes. (*Beat.*) Thank God things are looking up. She'll get this play. She's perfect. *Who's Afraid of Virginia Woolf?* It's one of my favourites.

Henry Is it?

Alec Certainly ... I saw it in the States once, with, oh, Jesus, what's that girl's name? God ... Elaine Stritch. That's the role Anne should be playing, given her temperament ... she should be playing that role.

(**Anne** *enters.*)

Anne What role?

20

Alec And here she is.

Anne I'm sorry for leaving you two together.

Alec There's no need to apologize for anything, Anne.

Anne On your own, I meant.

Alec How is your friend?

Anne (*ignoring this*) Henry, I'm sorry.

Henry I should have rung first?

Anne Maybe.

Alec (*smarmy*) He said he was just passing through this neighbourhood.

Henry (*getting up*) I am ... I'm sorry ...

Alec We've been confabulating agreeably.

Anne Never mind.

Alec Isn't she a card?

>   (*He touches her fondly, intimately. She reacts a bit.*
>   **Henry** *stares.* **Alec** *starts to exit.*)

I'm going to the rest-room.

Anne All right.

Alec Then we'll get down to business. Nice to see you, Henry. We'll have to trade stories, some time.

>   (*He exits.*)

Anne (*brusque*) I apologize for this. I forgot you were coming. This is a double booking.

Henry I don't really understand why it's so embarrassing. He could leave.

>   (*Pause.* **Anne** *doesn't look at him.*)

Can I stay, perhaps? I'll wait in the garden until you've finished.

Anne (*firm*) No. (*Beat.*) It's freezing outside.

Henry I don't like him, Anne. He's ... he's such a phoney.

>   (**Anne** *doesn't answer.* **Henry** *sighs. Beat.* **Henry** *is about to leave.*)

21

Anne How's your man?

Henry What?

Anne Your new man.

Henry He's ... (*smiles*) Good.

    (*Beat.*)

Anne Jesus, why can't he call it the loo like everyone else?

    (*Crossfade.*)

Scene 4

Outside **Trevor**'s *block of flats, Paddington. Late morning.* **Trevor** *is seen sitting on the steps to the main entrance as* **Henry** *enters.*

Henry Hi. Trevor?

Trevor Hey!

Henry Hello.

Trevor You came this time!

Henry Yeah.

    (*Beat.* **Trevor** *smiles.*)

Trevor I didn't know if you would.

Henry Here I am.

Trevor Didja get out at Paddington?

Henry Yeah.

Trevor Well, this is it. Shocking, isn't she? You do get a view of Hyde Park if you climb on the roof though. Ugliest building in W2.

    (*Beat.*)

Henry I like it ...

Trevor Nah, it's mediocre. Who'd live in Paddington, eh?

Henry You.

Trevor Yeah, me.

    (*Pause.*)

Henry *(awkward)* Are you ... going to take me in?

Trevor Nah. Not yet. Take a seat 'ere.

(Pause. **Henry** *sits.)*

I can keep check on life from here, yeah? *(gets out cigarettes)* Dodgy area, this. Too many cheap hotels, one after the other. Full of people who have just got off the boat, you know, or swum the channel. *(lights up)* Fag?

Henry No thanks.

(Pause. **Trevor** *looks about, smokes.)*

Trevor I used to live in that one.

Henry On the ground floor?

Trevor Yeah, but I 'ad to get out. I mean, it's not much better upstairs but you don't get people pissing on your window sills.

(Beat.)

Henry Cats.

Trevor Look at 'em all ... strays, all of 'em. Like a bloody ménage ... Psstt! Is that what I mean? No, a menagerie. Yeah, that's what I mean. Disgusting ... They're always half-moulted like that ... mangy, dirty bastard.

Henry They look hungry.

Trevor Well I'm not gonna feed 'em, they'll follow me up. There's no way I'm lettin' 'em in ... Suffer.

Henry Poor things.

Trevor Don't you start. All day they look up ... I get sick of 'em lookin' up at me. *(Beat.)* This feels weird. I don't do it like this, you know, usually. I mean usually I bring people straight back. But you, you're different. *(Beat.)* How long's it been now?

(Beat.)

Henry Four weeks.

Trevor Four weeks! I've known you for four weeks! Can't believe we 'aven't made it back 'ere in all that time.

Henry I was thinking of coming last night.

Trevor Yeah? It's for the best this way. I looked at you when I first saw you, I thought ... I would normally, straight away, bring you back ... but something told me to wait, I'll wait for you to see my joint when you're ready to see it. Four weeks! I'm kickin' myself!

Henry Well, I'm here now.

Trevor Good.

Henry It's nice.

   (*Beat.*)

Trevor Been here three years, maybe four, pretty lucky to get it really. Contacts, y'see? Someone once told me I'm the friendliest person in the block, you know. 'Er upstairs laughed 'er 'ead off.

Henry What — you do live with someone?

Trevor No. Her up there. (*points*) She lives in that one. Closest to the sky. She'll be on 'er backside now, painting or something.

Henry Oh.

Trevor Not 'er flat, she's an artist. Her name's Caroline. She takes no notice of me. Bitch. (*He looks up. Pause.*) I painted the walls Canadian lemon in mine a year back. But I didn't much like Canadian lemon in the end, so now they're coral-magnolia. Didn't tell the landlord. They're all crooks, land-lords. You eaten yet?

Henry No.

Trevor Good.

   (*Pause. They look at each other.*)

Caroline's middle-aged.

Henry Is she?

Trevor Yeah. It's amazing how many middle-agers I know, they're the only proper sort of people I seem to meet, actually.

Henry Well, age doesn't matter.

Trevor Nah. Every night you 'ear 'er mixing plaster for casts and that. She is the *queen* of plaster.

Henry Really?

Trevor Oh yeah. She's got no taste. Listens to Jackson Browne.

Henry Has she lived here long?

Trevor Years. It's amazing, but I've never seen a thing, not prop'ly ... not a paintin', not a sculpture, nothin'. She won't let me. (*Beat.*) She's got abnormal friends, Henry. From Notting Hill. She's got stuff in a gallery there.

Henry Well ... why don't you go in? Then you'd see some of her work.

Trevor No. No, I don't wanna go in there. No way. (*Beat.*) Do you think she's got any talent?

Henry (*surprised*) What?

Trevor Do you think she's got any talent?

Henry But I've never met her.

Trevor Yeah, well you will. (*Long pause.*) Well ...

Henry (*awkward*) Well ...

Trevor Henry. Great name. Royal, like.

Henry I suppose.

(*Beat.*)

Trevor I got somethin' in the oven.

Henry Oh.

Trevor Yeah. We'll go inside.

Henry All right then.

(*Beat.*)

Trevor Do they call you 'Arry?

Henry Never, no one.

Trevor Hen, then.

Henry Maybe.

Trevor (*smiles*) Good. (*stretches himself out on the steps*) Let's go up.

(*Pause. They are still sitting. Crossfade.*)

Scene 5

A square, near **Anne**'s *flat.* **Henry** *and* **Anne** *are sitting.*

Henry He's got more 501s than you could ever think possible, pairs and pairs of the bloody things ...

Anne I thought they were passé for gay men.

Henry I don't know, you're asking me? Anyway, it's against the by-laws of the building to hang washing out on the balconies but he says he doesn't give a shit about anything like that. "You've got to make the most of this good weather," he says ... so they hang there, it's like a Chinese laundry.

Anne It sounds a bit sordid.

Henry Yes, sordid. They've probably spent more time around his ankles than ... (*tails off*)

Anne Oh, he gets about?

Henry He gets about. His name is Trevor. He's completely strange.

Anne Trevor?

Henry Yes.

Anne I don't know any Trevors. (*Beat.*) I got the play.

Henry What?

Anne I got it. Remember that audition? I had two call-backs. They were cunts, Frappy, absolute cunts. They offered it to me yesterday.

Henry Anne! Congratulations! Why didn't you tell me? Before?

    (*They hug.*)

Anne I'm relieved.

Henry I bet. This is ... amazing. Well done.

Anne It's about time, Frappy.

Henry Oh, I know, but ... you've got it now. Where is it?

Anne Islington.

Henry Brilliant, it's what you've wanted.

Anne Yes, I know all that crap. (*Beat.*) It is about time, you see: say it. I've been out of work for ages. Say it's about time.

(*Beat.*)

Henry OK. It's about time.

(*Beat.*)

Anne But money's not a problem for me, is it? Say that.

Henry Anne, this is great news, you deserve it. I'm so excited ...

Anne Oh ... bloody platitudes. Money's not a problem. Say that.

Henry No.

Anne Damn, Henry ...

Henry I don't know, anyway, Anne. How should I know what your situation is? You've got work, this is ... let's celebrate ...

Anne I didn't go to drama school, Henry.

Henry So?

Anne I didn't go to Oxbridge or some other middle-class, recently accredited university, I didn't do all the things you're meant to do, to get work, and I ask myself, should I really feel right about this? ... When I see ... people like —

Henry (*interrupting*) Anne, I'm so happy for you, don't spoil it. Congratulations.

(*Pause.*)

Anne Thank you, Frappy.

Henry I'll help you with your lines.

Anne (*guffaws*) It's not the school play. (*Beat.*) Yes. Henry. (*Pause.*) What's this guy look like? He's the primitive one, isn't he? It is him.

Henry Yes. There's nothing in it ... he's simply ... He's not ... very attractive, if you must know.

Anne Yes, but has he got a nice ...? (*gestures*)

Henry He's got a pimply forehead. His nose and mouth are

27

always pouting, sort of, contorted into a snigger. He walks about ... appropriating everything.

(*Pause.*)

Anne I had grapefruit today.

Henry Did you?

Anne It went everywhere, dripped, all over my chest and all over the duvet cover.

Henry Bad luck.

Anne It was careless ... all over my brand new duvet cover. Then I spilled coffee on it as well. Still, a lovely big fat cheque bounced over the other day.

(*Uncomfortable pause, then they laugh.*)

Lucky me.

(**Anne** *looks away. Music. Crossfade.*)

Scene 6

One of the communal balconies of **Trevor***'s block of flats,* **Trevor***'s level.* **Caroline** *and* **Trevor** *are seen, drinking red wine and smoking, as* **Henry** *enters.*

Henry (*from the end of the balcony*) Hello?

Trevor Hen! Come and join us. Over here.

(**Henry** *walks to them.*)

There's a spare chair up against the wall.

Henry (*as he reaches them*) Hi.

Trevor Hi! Caroline's come down for a drink. For one of our balcony sessions. (*to* **Caroline**) This is Henry. Henry: Caroline.

Caroline I've seen you. You've been here quite a few times, haven't you?

Henry I suppose I have.

Caroline Hello anyway.

Henry Hello.

Caroline Better late than never.

Trevor Good.

(*Beat.*)

Caroline I come out to the balconies and I look down from above. I see everything.

Henry Right.

Trevor Nice evening for it, though, i'n't it ...? Dusk ... My favourite. We come out 'ere at dusk like the crickets do.

Henry It gets quite noisy around here, doesn't it?

Trevor Tourists comin' in and out of Paddington — everywhere. Continental delights. You stayin'?

Henry Thought I might.

Trevor Have a drink then.

Caroline It's Bulgarian. Do you want some?

Henry Oh, that's kind. I should have brought something ...

Trevor Henry, sit down ...

Henry (*to* **Caroline**, *as he takes the wine and sits*) Thank you.

Trevor We were just discussing, Henry, about movie stars. Caroline and me, we talk about movie stars a lot. Caroline goes for the older men, of course. I was saying, Winona Ryder is sexier and more talented than Sandra Bullock.

Caroline Trevor ...

Trevor Not a patch on Lady Sarah Chatto, though.

Caroline Who? Oh, for goodness sake.

Trevor Or Mr Chatto, come to that, what do you say, Hen?

Henry Er ...

Trevor Very dishy, both of them ... the only things worth anything in the whole sodding family.

(*Beat.*)

Caroline So, are you two ... ? (*indicates with her hands "a couple"*)

29

Trevor No ...

Henry No ... not ... really.

>   (**Trevor** *smiles*.)

Caroline (*casually*) Well, you're sensible.

Henry Why is that?

Caroline He isn't faithful to anyone.

>   (*Beat*.)

Henry Trevor ... ?

>   (**Trevor** *doesn't answer*.)

Caroline We all see him go out ... he returns late at night
with a stranger in tow, sometimes a woman, sometimes a
man. He thinks he's Joe Orton. The pick-up often stays all
night. But in the morning, the daytime light ekes its way into
Trevor's flat and it's insulting enough to reveal just how plain
he really is, and I see the pick-up walk regretfully down the
drive. Every time ...

>   (*Uncomfortable pause. They drink.*)

Trevor Quite a few of them go to this school down near
where my parents live, you know.

Caroline Who?

Trevor The royal family. Some of them do, I think.

Henry I thought you were from London.

Trevor My parents are on a dairy farm. In Dorset, near that
school ...

Henry Sherborne?

Trevor That's the one. Well, twenty minutes or so.

Henry (*surprised*) Oh.

Trevor Why the surprise?

>   (*Beat*.)

Henry Nothing. I thought you were from London.

Trevor Well I am really. Been 'ere long enough.

Caroline Perhaps it's time to go back?

Trevor Caroline's very parochial. She goes down to Westminster underground just to see the looks on tourists' faces as they come out and see Big Ben for the first time. She's been at work on a guidebook for years.

Henry Have you?

Trevor But she can't finish it.

Caroline I'm too busy with my art.

    (*Beat.*)

Henry What sort of guidebook?

Trevor It's called *The Tribes of London* ...

Caroline (*ignoring* **Trevor**) I'm trying to characterize the city in — yes, Trevor — a tribal sense.

Trevor Very anthropological it is.

Caroline How types of people ... have congregated ... creating, sort of, villages, with particular characteristics.

Trevor It's all about *ghettos*! She even includes Clapham, Hen!

Caroline Anyway, the point is, it stays unpublished.

Trevor I've got friends in publishing, from the factory. Perhaps they could help.

Caroline If you really did, you wouldn't be saying that.

Trevor She told me to go to Tesco's to buy myself an existence last week.

Caroline They were on special.

Henry I'm in publishing.

Caroline Are you?

Trevor I've never asked, you know, never even asked what you did.

Henry Just starting out, really.

Caroline An editor once told me my writing was too "ebullient", can you believe it, that was her very word.

Trevor I've seen it ... I saw some of the manuscript ...

Caroline A very small section, Trevor ...

Trevor Sought out the relevant bits, eh? (*to* **Henry**) Old Compton Street! There's a chapter about Paddington.

Caroline Paddington! Hah, there's nothing in Paddington.

Trevor What about you Hen, were you born here?

Henry No ... not a real Londoner.

Trevor None of us are, none of us.

Caroline There's too much here for the tourists.

Trevor (*confidentially; mocking*) You've got to live amongst the tribes.

Caroline (*to* **Henry**) He's too busy with other things, like personal gratification, to even begin contemplating the beauty, or non-beauty, of his surroundings ... he's a greenhorn here, a greenhorn back on the farm, a greenhorn everywhere. Don't take any notice of *anything* Trevor says.

Trevor She loves me ...

Caroline Yes. Absolutely. I have work to do. (*finishes her wine*) Nice to meet you, Henry. Bye-bye.

Henry Bye.

　　　　(**Caroline** *exits.*)

She's very attractive.

Trevor I know.

Henry Why does she live here?

Trevor What do you mean?

Henry She's not suited to these flats, not like you ... or, or, or me even.

Trevor Because she walks about the place as if she was this mega-successful artist?

Henry Well, yeah.

Trevor What a put-on.

Henry Maybe it's not.

Trevor It is.

Henry I can picture her at the opening of an exhibition in a

32

small art gallery — sipping champagne under the bright spotlights.

Trevor Yeah. (*Beat.*) She's gone upstairs to work. She does it every evenin'. Cue Jackson Browne. (*Beat.*) And then she goes out. I'm not the only one. She goes out too.

Henry Do you mind?

Trevor No. (*Beat.*) I see 'er. I see 'er trundle down the road with 'er purple batik sling-bag over 'er shoulder and 'er flowers and 'er bottle of wine ... (*Beat.*) She's 'avin' an affair with a priest.

Henry Really.

Trevor Oh, yeah. She won't talk about it, but I know.

Henry How?

Trevor I spied on 'er once.

Henry What?

Trevor I spied on 'er. Dark glasses, other side of the road, that sort of thing. Done it a few times.

(*Beat.*)

Henry Why did you do that?

Trevor Because I did. (*Beat.*) We'll go out. (*Beat.*) I've just got to go back inside ... to get ready, like. (*Beat.*) We'll go out.

(*Long pause. They sit and drink. Crossfade.*)

Scene 7

A West End night-club, just before closing. Flashing lights, loud music. **Henry** *and* **Trevor** *are on the periphery.* **Henry** *has a Budweiser.* **Trevor** *has a bottle of Evian. He is very drunk.*

Trevor I kept my promise.

Henry Yes, you kept your promise.

Trevor To see you through till the evenin' is out.

Henry I think that's about now. Look, Trevor, I've really had enough. Can we go?

Trevor Maybe not next time, though, eh? Next time we'll make a different sort of promise! (*looking out over the dance floor*) Comin'?

Henry No, I think it's time ... It closes soon. (*looks at his watch, taps it*) Four-thirty.

Trevor I'm out there ...

> (**Trevor** *dances, centre.* **Henry** *looks on hopelessly.* **Trevor** *comes back to* **Henry**, *still dancing.*)

Henry Look at you!

Trevor Can't stop, 'ave to keep moving. It's called "Bill and Coo" on Sunday nights. Goes all queeny.

Henry Does it?

Trevor It's fantastic. I love all that shit. My friend Moana, you'll 'ave to meet 'er.

Henry Yeah.

Trevor I thought you probably wouldn't 'ave been here. I sized you up, and I thought, where can I take 'im where 'e 'asn't been?

Henry Well, we've done it now.

Trevor It's a bit different from where we met, eh? Yeah. I come here on and off, actually. It's my safe haven if you know what I mean. Always lots of pretty boys, a few pretty girls. (*dances; offers a popper*) Popper?

Henry Er, no thanks.

Trevor (*offers his drink*) Evian?

Henry (*accepts*) Thanks.

Trevor You needed that, hey? Gets hot in 'ere.

Henry Damn hot.

> (**Trevor** *is moving to the music. They both look out over the dance floor.*)

Trevor I've been told that I excel on the dance floor, that's what somebody said, that I excelled! See anything you like?

Henry What?

Trevor (*looking off*) Now that's a nice face ... see that guy, pull him your way! He was ugly at the bar, I saw 'im, but out there!

Henry Out there ...

Trevor Out there he could pull John Major.

(*They watch.*)

Henry ... four-thirty ...

Trevor Yeah.

Henry Come on, then.

Trevor All right, Henry. All right, mate.

(*They move off.*)

Henry Should we get a taxi? It'd be easier. Trevor?

Trevor (*takes a sniff of the popper*) Come 'ere.

(*He pulls* **Henry** *towards him roughly and kisses him, passionately. It lasts a while.*)

You're great. (*Beat.*) Yeah.

(*Beat.*)

Henry Trevor?

Trevor Yeah. What? No taxis, no. I may be smashed, but I'm not gullible. (*drunkenly*) Taxi drivers, wise to the, to the ... malleability ... yeah ... of drunk and drugged clubbers. Well I'm not danced-out! I'm walking home!

Henry Trevor, I'll walk you to the bus.

Trevor No! Come on.

(*They walk away from the club. The music fades.*)

Trevor Here begins the new life!

Henry What?

Trevor Here begins the new life!

(*He runs his fingers through his hair, loses his balance and falls to the ground.*)

Henry Trevor ...

Trevor Here *beginneth* the new life!

Henry What are you talking about, Trevor ...? How are you getting home?

Trevor Bus.

Henry Come on then.

Trevor Where to?

Henry Trafalgar Square.

Trevor Follow me.

Henry What?

Trevor Let's go this way.

Henry Are you sure?

Trevor This way!

Henry OK, OK.

(*They begin to walk.*)

Trevor ...?

Trevor (*mumbling and declaiming, to whomever will listen*) Caroline ... and all those goddamn geraniums ... new life ... in a desert by the Nile ... crocodile ... saw a smile ... for a while ... over a stile ... got a pile ... eat some bile ... "Edgware Poetry Society"! Henry!

Henry What?

Trevor (*making a sign in the air*) "Edgware Poetry Society". That's me!

Henry Trevor ...

Trevor "Edgware Poetry Society ... present an evening of new poetry by young writers." Me!

Henry What ...? Where does it say that, Trevor?

Trevor All over London! Billboards plastered everywhere. Last year. Me! I did a reading of some of my poetry there. At the Poets' Warehouse in Lisson Grove.

Henry Poetry?

Trevor Poetry!

Henry You write poetry?

Trevor Of course I do! I'm the Bard of Sussex Gardens, if not the whole of Paddington!

> (**Trevor** *shouts, over and over, "Me" and then, out of breath, he sits on the ground.*)

(*mumbling*) And there I left you, sitting on the hedge ... Abandoning our marriage pledge ... (*smiles*) Here begins the new life ... (*shuts his eyes*)

Henry Trevor?

Trevor Here begins the new life ...

Henry Oh. Fuck.

Trevor Goodnight.

> (**Trevor** *sleeps. Music. Crossfade.*)

Scene 8

A party. Music. Lots of people. **Henry** *and* **Anne** *stand, drinking.* **Henry** *is a little drunk; he holds a glass and a bottle of wine.*

Henry (*looking off*) Look who's here.

Anne I know. We came together, actually.

Henry Oh.

Anne Don't be surprised. I owe him.

Henry Why?

Anne It doesn't matter. I let him mix with me socially once in a while. It makes things easier. Although I didn't know you were going to be here.

Henry Yes you did.

Anne I forgot. Anyway, how's your friend?

Henry What?

Anne The boy called Trevor.

Henry Fine.

Anne Fine. Just fine?

Henry Yes.

Anne I should meet him.

Henry No, no. Not ... yet.

Anne It's been ages.

Henry Later.

Anne Why? (*Beat.*) What does he do? What? (*Beat.*) What? I'm intrigued.

>   (*Beat.*)

Henry I met the artist who lives above him, Caroline.

Anne So ... ?

Henry Well ... he has a thing for her. (*Beat.*) This isn't bad, this party ...

Anne Henry ...

>   (*Pause.*)

Henry The other day we went to Notting Hill and we ended up spying on this Caroline.

Anne You're kidding.

Henry No. She drinks coffee with her friends opposite this gallery that sells some of her sculptures. We walked up and down the street all morning, *spying*.

Anne Why?

Henry To keep check on her, see what she's doing. He hates the way she holds her cappuccino, he hates her twittering friends.

Anne Doesn't she see him?

Henry She spotted us once, I'm sure.

Anne What did she do?

Henry Ignored us ... Trevor's not what you'd call Notting Hill chic.

Anne It's almost sad, Frappy ... the poor man.

Henry Yeah, well. Anyway, he calls them "Geraniums".

Anne Who?

Henry Caroline's friends. It's his code word. He can't bear them because they're so cold, unapproachable. Here. I've brought this. (*gets out some of* **Trevor's** *poetry*) This is his revenge.

Anne What?

Henry Bad poetry.

Anne (*reads*) "Note their hard profiles, their inflated crani- ums / As they sit and sip their *caffe-latte* / Suits by Gaultier, watches by Cartier / These over-watered, stiff Geraniums." He writes this stuff?

Henry Yeah, he says he's a poet ... he's done readings. What do you think ...?

Anne He's a nut-case.

Henry I like him. I really like him.

(*Beat.*)

Anne (*teasing*) Poetry.

Henry Yes.

Anne Poetry ...! Has he written an epic in honour of you?

Henry Anne.

Anne Well ... (*Beat.*) I must meet him. It's as simple as that.

Henry We'll see.

Anne What about this woman though? What's his real — persuasion?

(*Pause.*)

Henry It's part of his ... charm. He — collects people.

Anne And where does that leave you?

(*Beat.*)

39

Henry Do you want another drink?

    (*But there's none left.*)

Anne I shouldn't be too late.

    (*They stand for a while, drinking, moving to the music.*)

Henry (*looking off*) Alec's loving it.

Anne (*likewise*) Poor girl.

Henry Who is she?

Anne Some inbred heifer.

Henry I haven't seen him since your place, that day.

Anne Don't harp on that again. It was unintended.

Henry Imagine, me sitting in your living-room. *On my own.* Talking to the dreaded Alec for more than three minutes.

Anne (*sarcastic*) Sorry about that. (*blasé*) Must've been hell.

Henry It was very enlightening.

Anne Henry. I don't care what you think, or even what you know.

    (*Pause. She looks off.*)

Henry You've got lines to learn now, I suppose.

Anne What?

Henry Your lines ... for the play.

Anne Oh ... something like that.

Henry Can I do anything?

Anne No. (*smiles*) You're too busy anyway ... with your poet from Paddington.

    (*Beat.*)

Henry Look at him — he's doing the rounds. (*Beat.*) It's funny how you don't want us to be together.

Anne Codswallop. Subject change.

    (*Beat.*)

Henry I think he's like an anteater, something prickly: he'd bristle if you touched him. Of course, we've got to think of the

40

American equivalent of an anteater, or are anteaters American?

Anne Frappy ...

Henry An armadillo?

Anne I don't care at the moment.

Henry Where do porcupines live?

Anne Henry, please be quiet ...

Henry Anne ...?

Anne I'm going to get a drink now.

Henry Get one for me, would you?

Anne You don't need one.

Henry But I do.

> (**Anne** *exits.* **Henry** *stands, looking around. He moves to the music. Pause.* **Alec** *enters behind* **Henry** *and taps him on the shoulder. He has a bottle of wine.*)

Alec Hello!

Henry Oh. (*looks off in* **Anne**'s *direction*) Hello, Alec.

Alec What an enjoyable party!

Henry I suppose.

Alec Anne's left you here, on your own?

Henry No.

Alec No? Charming. (*Beat.*) So.

Henry So.

> (*Beat.*)

Alec All right for a drink?

Henry Yes. Thanks. I've had a bit too much, if you want the truth.

Alec So what have you two been up to?

Henry Excuse me?

Alec You and Anne. Been up to much lately?

Henry No, not really.

Alec You're very tight, you two, aren't you.

Henry (*laughs*) Are you grilling me?

Alec No, I'm making conversation, Henry.

(*Beat.*)

Henry We're, we're close ... I rely on her, she on me ...

Alec That's so sweet ...

(*Beat.*)

Henry I like to think it's because — we're not the same.

Alec Uhuh.

Henry I think most of her friends are ... (*looking around*) ... Sloanes — well you're not one obviously ... Anyway, I'm a little different.

Alec You each fill a void in the other's life.

Henry Yes. No. I suppose you might say that.

Alec A Sloane antidote. Imagine that. You should market the concept. Are you in love with her?

(*Beat.*)

Henry (*serious*) I can't answer that.

Alec Aren't you ...? How can I put this delicately? ... Don't you shop at a different department store?

(*Beat.* **Henry** *looks at him warily, then laughs.*)

Henry I could ask the same thing of you.

Alec Go ahead.

(**Henry** *laughs, shyly. Pause.*)

Henry Do you ... shop at a different department store?

Alec From you I think I do. Or, maybe not.

(**Henry** *laughs, unsure.* **Alec** *fills up their glasses from the bottle.*)

Don't you have someone new, now? Aren't you seeing someone? A new man friend?

(*Pause.*)

42

Henry No, I'm not. (*drinks most of the glass*)

Alec Do you love her?

Henry Of course.

Alec Sexually?

(*He refills **Henry**'s glass. Pause. **Henry** drinks.*)

Henry I ... I ... (*Long pause. He breathes heavily.*) The other day we were out ... at night ... we were walking around Clapham at night. And Anne collected some pebbles, and as if she was bowling, she rolled them down the road. She made clicking noises with her mouth. They rolled over the bitumen and her laughter echoed up into the night — and all I wanted to do Alec ... (*Pause.*) ... was fuck her.

(**Alec** *smiles.*)

Why are you smiling?

(**Alec** *says nothing. He drinks.*)

You shouldn't be smiling. No ...

Alec (*teasingly, almost flirtatious*) Shouldn't I, why not? You felt like ... (*laughs*) ... fucking her ...

Henry (*timidly*) Yes.

Alec That might be funny ... some people would consider it a laughing matter.

(*He laughs. **Henry** laughs with him.*)

Henry Would they? I don't know ... (*Pause.*) That's what I wanted to do — this urge came over me, but, but I didn't want to seduce her, Alec, I wanted to do it there in the street.

Alec (*laughing*) There, in the street?

Henry Yeah.

Alec In the middle of Clapham?

Henry Yeah.

Alec Goodness, you kill me.

(**Henry** *bursts into laughter.*)

Henry I can hardly explain it, you know. This hedonistic sexual feeling for her came over me ...

Alec Well, I know, I've been there ...

Henry (*not taking this in, continuing*) Yeah ... as powerful as any urge I've ever had. It's a heinous thought, I thought ...

Alec Heinous ... (*laughs*)

Henry ... wanting to make love to her here right now, in the street ...

Alec ... in Clapham ...

Henry ... in Clapham, but I can't — couldn't — help it. "Anne," I wanted to say ... "Can't we just forget all this ..." I don't know, "Propriety", "Our lives", whatever it is ... "Can't we just cut all of this and have each other *right here*!"

Alec Right here!

> (*They laugh, and drink, and look at each other. The laughing subsides.*)

Henry Why is this funny?

Alec Because look at you.

Henry What?

Alec Well, you *do* shop at the other department store, n'est-ce-pas? (*very threatening*) You worship in the other chapel, yes? Surf an alternative Internet, bat for the other team, bark up a different tree, row a different boat, dance to a different tune? (*Pause.*) You play Twister without the ladies? (*Beat.*) Never mind, you were saying.

Henry Um ...

Alec So, what happened?

Henry Nothing. Of course, nothing happened. We, we sang. Just outside the tube station ... near that fenced-off bit where there are daffodils in spring ...

> (*Pause.* **Henry** *drinks. Pause. He sings a snatch of "Giants in the Sky" from* Into the Woods, *plaintively, sad.*)

Alec Oh, yes, that.

(**Henry** *sings a bit more. Beat.*)

Henry (*uneasy, drunk*) We both knew the words. We thought it was very urbane. And when we finished, we sang a medley of Carpenters' hits, which was not quite as sophisticated but still hip, retrospectively. She left me there. 1.30 a.m. A black cab was going north. That never happens. "Bye, Frappy," she called. "See you tomorrow!"

Alec And you went home?

(*Pause.*)

Henry No.

Alec You were just near Clapham Common?

Henry Yes.

Alec Well that's convenient for a fuck.

Henry Yes. (*Beat.*) Hey, fuck you.

(**Alec** *laughs.* **Henry** *stares at him, alarmed. Music. Crossfade.*)

Scene 9

Outside **Trevor's** *flat.* **Henry** *and* **Trevor** *are sitting on the steps to the main entrance.* **Trevor** *is stretched out, soaking up the sun, smoking.* **Henry** *reads.*

Trevor (*languid*) In a desert by the Nile ... (*Beat.*) I saw an angel smile a smile ... (*Beat.*) What you think of that? (*Beat.*) Yeah. Smile a smile. (*Beat.*) Hen?

Henry Great.

(*Beat.*)

Trevor It made me think of hugging trees. And brought me crashing to my knees ... (*Beat.*) Yeah.

(*Sound of a car.* **Trevor** *looks up as it drives past.* **Henry** *keeps reading.*)

Who's this? Not seen this one before. Green Renault. M759ADP.

Henry What?

Trevor Nothing. (*Beat*) Hugging trees. No. (*looks off*) Holy McFoley, watch it! — Jesus!

(*Crash!* **Henry** *looks up.*)

Henry What's going on?

Trevor (*over this; getting up*) Straight into it!

Henry (*overlapping*) What's happened —?

Trevor (*overlapping*) She drove straight into it! Bloody hell, look at that! Didn't even see it!

Henry I don't believe it ...

Trevor Look, look, some nutter's driven into Caroline's scarecrow!

(**Anne** *enters, holding a piece of tin. She carries a Harrods' bag.*)

Henry Anne!

Trevor Did you see what you did! Straight into it!

Anne Excuse me, Frappy, what's that ridiculous thing back there?

Henry What are you doing here?

Anne I followed you. What's this?

Henry (*distracted*) It's a sculpture.

Trevor Caroline's scarecrow! (*bursts into laughter*) You've hit the scarecrow!

Anne A scarecrow?

Henry (*sotto voce*) Thank God she's not here.

Trevor (*still laughing*) Look what you've done! Pranged right into the scarecrow!

(*He runs off to have a look.*)

Anne Is he serious?

Henry Yes ... right into Ray Bolger.

(**Trevor** *runs back on with another piece.*)

Trevor Yeah ... yeah ... "We're off to see the wizard ..." (*bursts into laughter*)

Henry It's a scarecrow, of sorts ... it's art ... you know ... Caroline's, the artist, she lives upstairs. What are you doing here?

Anne A scarecrow ...?

Henry Yes.

Anne Made from ... this?

Henry (*cross*) Yes. Sheets of tin, pipes and bits of an old push-bike. Caroline usually takes to welding on a new part at the weekends if the weather is nice. Very Turner Prize.

Trevor It'll probably win now!

Henry There have been complaints but I don't think it can be moved.

Anne Oh dear. (*holding up the tin*) This came off, Frappy.

Trevor It's the flag, you know, the pennant! The flag the scarecrow was holding!

Henry How's your car?

Anne Not a scratch.

Trevor Ha!

Anne Oh well.

Henry Yes, don't worry about it, now.

Anne OK, I won't.

> (*She moves towards* **Henry** *and gives him a kiss; she looks at* **Trevor**)

Hello, Frappy darling. I've brought poppy seed rolls and cream cheese. We can go and sit in Hyde Park, it's just around the corner, I drove straight past it!

Henry But how ...?

Anne I can't stay long though, I'm bloody busy, the play opens soon.

Henry (*to himself*) Oh, God.

47

(**Trevor** *stands, fascinated by* **Anne**.)

I wasn't expecting you.

Anne I found the address on your telephone table.

Henry You were snooping?

Anne It's not snooping.

Henry I don't believe you ...

Anne Come on, let's eat quickly. I'm starving.

(*She pauses, then looks at* **Trevor**)

Your friend can come too.

Henry Um, Anne, this is Trevor, he lives here. Trevor: Anne.

Trevor Hello, Anne. Hen's mentioned you.

Anne (*instantly flirtatious*) Mmm, he's mentioned you too, once or twice.

Trevor You're an actress then?

Anne (*all smiles*) An actor. Yes, I am. Sometimes.

Trevor And you're in a play, then?

Anne Yes.

Trevor Which one?

Anne It's called *Who's Afraid of Virginia Woolf?*

Trevor Edward Albee. Won the Pulitzer Prize.

Anne Do you know it?

Trevor Sure, sure. There's the film, i'n't there? Are you playing Honey?

Anne (*impressed*) Yes. It's the role that Sandy —

Trevor (*interrupts, excited*) Sandy Dennis played her, I know ... I love that film. (*Pause.*) You'll be perfect!

(*Pause.* **Trevor** *stares at* **Anne**. *They smile at each other.* **Henry** *looks uncomfortable.* **Anne** *sighs happily.*)

I'll 'ave to come and see it.

Anne Why don't you? Please.

(*Beat.*)

Trevor I've done some acting.

Anne Have you? We all do at some stage, don't we ...?

Trevor (*staring at her*) Yeah ... I was Hansel once, I sang a song called "I'm your big brother, I must take the place of Dad and Mother".

Anne Did you steal the show?

Trevor (*laughing*) I reckon I did! Mum's still waiting for me to crack Hollywood, but!

>   (**Anne** *laughs. Pause.*)

Anne Well. You must come with us. Trevor.

Trevor No, no, I couldn't.

Anne Oh, please come.

Trevor No, I can't.

Anne Why not?

Trevor I'm goin' out later on.

Henry Are you?

Trevor Yeah.

Henry Where?

Anne Oh, what a shame.

Henry Where are you going?

Trevor Things on, you know. (*Pause.*) I suppose I could cancel it.

Anne Try to. I should have met you ages ago, I want to get to know you better.

Trevor Yeah, likewise, smashing.

>   (*He smiles. No one moves.*)

Wait then! I'll do it! One quick phone-call and I'll be back.

Anne Good!

>   (**Trevor** *exits into the flats slowly, looking back at* **Anne.**)

What the dickens, Fraps? So this is where he lives?

Henry You know full well.

Anne It was clever of me to discover it ... admit it. (*Pause.*) He's fascinating.

Henry What are you doing here? I told you ... this is pretty damn intrusive, Anne.

Anne Stop being ridiculous, I had to meet him: you were never going to introduce him to me. (*looking after* **Trevor**) He's a strange boy. Low. A curious mixture. Very, very cute buns.

Henry Anne!

Anne Well?

(*Beat.*)

Henry He's not all he appears.

Anne I don't doubt it. I hope he likes Gorgonzola.

(**Henry** *looks at her. Pause.* **Trevor** *returns with a bottle.*)

Trevor I got out of it!

Anne Wonderful!

Trevor And I found a bottle of Bucks Fizz!

Anne (*smiles*) Well ... Hyde Park, it's so close, you lucky thing.

Trevor Yeah ... it's blinding.

Anne Shall we go, then?

Henry Snared.

Anne What?

Henry (*angrily*) I said snared.

Anne Who?

Henry All of us.

Anne (*to* **Trevor**) Take no notice of Henry, Trevor. He's a grump-pot.

(**Trevor** *and* **Anne** *look at each other, smiling. Music. Crossfade.*)

Scene 10

Henry's *flat, Clapham. Bookcases. CDs.* **Henry** *and* **Trevor**. **Trevor** *stands, looking around.*

Trevor I've never seen this place in the daylight.

Henry (*laughing*) Don't say that, Trevor.

Trevor It's not that bad.

Henry It is — I don't like it much. Hang on, I'll make some coffee.

(*He does so throughout the following.*)

Trevor White with three sugars. You shouldn't let it get you down.

Henry I can't help it. If I earned more money, I could afford somewhere nice, and I could live on my own — I'd prefer that.

Trevor You've got heaps of books.

Henry Some of them are Martin's. I've flipped through most of them.

Trevor Perhaps I should buy a few books like these. Here, I could borrow some.

Henry Why not? Fine.

Trevor It's nice stuff ... all of this ... I like it. (*Pause.*) Great CDs.

Henry Thanks.

Trevor The Beatles, Sarah Vaughan, opera, opera. Opera. Bit of an opera queen, eh? Nothing really contemporary.

Henry No.

Trevor Judy Garland.

Henry Yeah.

Trevor *Lots* of Judy Garland: box sets!

Henry Yes.

Trevor You know what that means.

Henry Yes, Trevor, it's, ah, it's an old joke.

Trevor I like *Little Nellie Kelly* best. Philip Glass.

Henry They're promotional copies. I got them for free.

Trevor No kidding?

Henry Anne gave them to me and they've just been sitting there for months ...

Trevor Anne!

Henry Yeah.

Trevor Now, I meant to say to you a few weeks ago ... she is something else ... I like her.

Henry Yeah.

Trevor She's a top-notch bird, that one.

Henry (*dismissive*) I've known her for a long time ... she's, she's an old friend.

Trevor I really like her, she's drop-dead. (*Beat.*) So she gives you free CDs and all? (*Beat.*) Industry contacts, I suppose.

   (*Pause.*)

Henry Sorry, did you say white?

Trevor Yeah. (*Pause.*) How do you know her?

Henry Anne?

Trevor Yeah.

Henry Old friend. We met up a few years ago.

Trevor You bumped into 'er at the theatre, di'n'cha?

Henry How did you know that?

   (*Beat.*)

Trevor We've been out.

   (*Beat.*)

Henry Who?

Trevor Anne and me. I didn't mean to lie or anything.

Henry You've been out with her?

Trevor Yeah.

Henry Why?

Trevor Don't know why I didn't say anythin'. Just didn't. She's asked me out again too. She's asked me to the openin' night of her play.

Henry But how did you ... find her?

Trevor She rang me up.

>(**Henry** *looks at him.*)

I ... er ... slipped 'er me phone number.

Henry Oh.

Trevor You don't mind?

>(*Beat.* **Henry** *doesn't answer.*)

We can talk for hours — she's got some wicked sense of humour you know. (*Beat.*) We talked about you. You two are pretty close, aren'tcha?

Henry Some of the time.

Trevor She's great.

>(*Beat.*)

Henry Where did you go?

Trevor Out and about. I don't think they're the sort of dives you'd normally get to.

Henry Meaning?

Trevor Not really your sport, see.

>(*Pause.* **Henry** *is annoyed. He looks off.*)

Henry She's pampered and out of touch. Her parents — they're not around any more — were very rich ...

Trevor Lucky her.

Henry She has ... a sugar daddy sort of figure. In her life.

Trevor A what?

Henry Sugar daddy. Someone who looks after her, financially, anyway. I'm not sure where he comes from, she's never told me.

Trevor A sugar daddy?

Henry Yes.

Trevor I need one of those.

Henry I see her ... all the time.

Trevor Yeah, well I really liked 'er — we should all go out, together.

> (*Pause.* **Henry** *hands him a cup of coffee, still annoyed.*)

Henry Here's your coffee.

Trevor Cheers.

Henry Sweet enough?

Trevor (*smiles*) Perfect.

> (*Pause.* **Henry** *sits.*)

I'll just settle down here.

> (*He sits down next to* **Henry** *and drinks his coffee. Pause.* **Trevor** *slowly goes to* **Henry** *and kisses him, tenderly, softly.* **Henry** *resists, then gives in. It lasts for a while.*)

We'll go out ourselves later, what do yer think?

Henry All right.

Trevor It's a good area, this. We'll go to the Two Brewers, see what's on offer.

Henry (*nodding*) Yeah.

Trevor I did well there the other night, you know.

Henry What night was that?

Trevor "The other night", you know, ages ago. You weren't around. He was a knockout.

> (*Pause.* **Henry** *looks into his coffee.* **Trevor** *kisses him again, shorter this time.*)

My writing's really coming along these past few weeks. I'm in the middle of this first-class cycle right now.

Henry Really?

Trevor Oh, yeah — you can read it soon. I'm a bit stuck on poem number four though. I've been trying to describe the look of the inside of this bordello, it's a place not far from here ... though I don't s'pose you'd know it.

Henry What?

Trevor I know it's a bit seedy, but you know how it is ... Anyway, this ... (*emphasizing it*) ... den of iniquity, as they say, is like brilliantly decorated in all this gold stuff, on the walls, you know what I mean?

Henry Does this make good poetry, Trevor? Really?

Trevor It's what all the great literature is about: Burroughs and the Beats, mate, even Shakespeare. Do you remember we were talkin', ages ago, about that chick up my way? It all started then. She was good, you know, source material ... Look: there's all this gold stuff on the walls, I need a word ... to describe it ... something ... *decadent.*

Henry How about ... "rococo"?

Trevor What?

Henry I don't know ... it could be rococo, I suppose.

Trevor Rococo?

Henry Yeah. Rococo. Is it?

Trevor What?

Henry Rococo?

Trevor I could make it.

Henry Well, there you go.

Trevor Rococo. Yeah.

(**Henry** *laughs.*)

I bet every good writer in the land has used the word "rococo" at least once, what do you reckon?

Henry So I've heard.

Trevor Yeah. Thanks, Hen. You're brilliant. Rococo. I bet it's just what I'm lookin' for.

Henry I hope it is.

Trevor Great stuff, wordsmith.

Henry Any time.

Trevor Hah! (*sips*) Good coffee.

Henry I get it from Brixton Market.

Trevor Brixton! Now, have I had some go-through-the-motions-experiences there!

(*Beat.*)

Henry Trevor, have you ever thought about ...? (*Beat.*) It doesn't matter.

Trevor No, go on.

(*Beat.*)

Henry Well: repercussions.

Trevor Repercussions?

Henry You're so quickly obsessed with things. People. Then you drop them, and I was just thinking about ...

Trevor It keeps me clean.

(*Beat.*)

Henry (*shaking his head; quizzically, upset*) Trevor.

Trevor What?

Henry Picking people up.

Trevor You do it.

Henry Yeah. But.

(*Beat.*)

Trevor (*seriously*) You're different, you know.

Henry It's almost as if you ... collect bits and pieces. Of strangers' souls.

Trevor That's deep. That's poetry, that is. I'll 'ave to remember that. (*sips; softly*) You're not a stranger, Henry.

Henry (*quickly; desperately, tearfully*) God. God.

Trevor What?

Henry You must know someone ... somebody: who's died.

Trevor Nah, mate. No one. (*Beat.*) Hen, baby. (*finishes his coffee*) Let's go out.

(*Music. Crossfade.*)

56

Scene 11

Anne's *flat. Sunday evening, late.* **Henry** *and* **Anne**. *Bottle of wine, lit candles on the floor. Mozart. The floor is covered in wrapping paper, cards, smart gifts — candlesticks, candles, teapots, vases, picture frames, bottles and jars of fruit, etc.* **Anne** *is busy, in her element, throughout.*

Anne It's all confusion, look. Thank heavens you're here.

Henry You'll be all right.

Anne Henry, only one more performance to go before the bastards ...

Henry You're amazingly nervous.

Anne I'm not nervous.

Henry You are.

Anne I'm not: just ... fucking overwrought. Thank you, *thank* you —

Henry (*over this*) It's all right.

Anne — for coming, I needed you.

    (*Beat.*)

Henry I'm yours. Till you want me to go. (*Beat.*) Here, I've brought this.

Anne What is it?

Henry A present.

Anne Oh dear, another one. Look around you. It's present city. First-night gifts, I won't get a chance to wrap them if I don't do it now. Put it over there, I'll open it later. No don't, I might give it to someone. Here ... Or shall I wait till Tuesday?

    (**Henry** *gives her the present.*)

Henry Break a leg.

    (**Anne** *opens the present. It's a carriage clock. She is shocked.*)

Anne Oh ... oh, goodness. It's divine ... (*Beat.*) Golly.

(*She puts the clock down. Long pause.*)

Have a look outside the window at my rhododendron. I've done nothing to it. Not one iota of green in my fingers yet look at it. She's a bloody marvel.

(*Beat. She looks at the clock, then picks it up. She looks at* **Henry** *and kisses him on the cheek.*)

Thank you.

(*She admires the clock again, then puts it down. Beat.*)

Henry You don't have one. (*Beat.*) Is it inappropriate?

Anne It's gorgeous, I love it. Thank you. (*Beat. She bustles.*) Are you drinking? There's wine open.

Henry I can't, I drove.

Anne Did you? Whose car?

Henry Martin's.

Anne Mine's playing up, otherwise I would have come and got you. It's very late ...

Henry It's all right, Anne.

Anne Is it?

Henry Yes.

Anne (*smiles*) There's a thing in my stomach, right here. I spent the day pootling, and now it's hit me.

Henry I wouldn't worry about it, it's healthy.

Anne Are you sure you don't want to come tomorrow night?

Henry What?

Anne As well as the opening? Please, I need to know how it's looking.

Henry I'm sure it's brilliant. I won't make any difference.

Anne I think it's booked out anyway. (*Beat.*) I could squeeze you in. Please come.

Henry Let me enjoy the opening, Anne. Surprise me. (*Beat.*) I'll see you then. Tuesday.

(**Anne** *gets to work. She finishes wrapping something.*)

Anne And you're coming to the party?

Henry Yes.

Anne It'll be very actory.

Henry I bet. Who else will I know — ?

Anne (*interrupts*) Come here, come here. I need your help. Hold that while I cut.

> (**Henry** *holds the present while she cuts the string. She offers him a drink again.*)

Wine?

Henry No. Thanks. Will Alec be there?

Anne Yes, he'll be there, Henry — he's always somewhere. (*Beat.*) Wine?

Henry No.

Anne I'll have some.

Henry This bottle?

Anne Yes. Any of them.

> (*She eats from a jar.*)

Henry So tell me all about it ...

Anne Excuse me, I'm eating a present. I'm starving hungry. What a day. The Sunday before and I go trotting off to Brighton, God knows why. Then I had to get back double quick for dinner at some self-important restaurant.

Henry Who with?

Anne Oh, the producer, who's too fat. I've only just got home. Sun-dried tomatoes. Have some. Go on.

Henry Aren't they for someone?

Anne It's only some lighting technician who wants my babies. Eat.

Henry Yum.

Anne Indeed. Yum. (*starts wrapping another present*) There's probably some balsamic vinegar amongst that lot if you want that too.

Henry Looks like you've spent a fortune.

Anne On credit. I'm poor as a church mouse. (*finishes wrapping*) Where's the raffia?

Henry This?

Anne Yes. Lovely. (*ties the present with raffia*) Bum-di-bum-bum. Comfy?

Henry Yeah ... fine.

Anne Here. Finger.

Henry What?

Anne Finger.

Henry Oh.

Anne And ... hold ... while I tie ... yes ... yes ... keep it there. OK. Extract. Good. Thank you. Thank you. This is for her-who's-playing-the-lead.

Henry Oh right — I saw her in the paper.

Anne (*with present*) Damn. I wish it would curl. There. She looked haggard, yes?

Henry That's all right, isn't it? For the role.

Anne Yes. Could you pass me a card — over there ...

Henry Here?

Anne (*looks up*) No, one of those Botticellis. (*as she works*) She's a real cow though. I would be too, I suppose. If it was my comeback role. How does that look? Pen?

Henry Here.

Anne (*as she writes on the card*) They're either going to come out saying, "That was the most gobsmackingly amazing thing I've seen" or, and this is looking more likely, "That. Was someone pulling my leg. And having a fucking good laugh about it." You look parched. I've got soft drinks. What do you want?

Henry Orange juice?

Anne Sorry, only prune. (*attaches the card*) There, how does that look?

Henry Lovely. Love the paper.

Anne Yes. As long as it looks good on the outside ... as they say. Now this ... (*a candlestick*) ... this is for my new friend, my very, very good-looking, very gay friend. He's playing my husband.

Henry It's beautiful.

Anne Candlesticks like this are common as mud, but never mind.

Henry Oh.

Anne Maroon tissue-paper, I think. Over there. Thank you. And ... there ... Sellotape. Two pieces. You're tremendous.

(*She works; he watches.*)

Change the music if you like.

Henry This is nice. (*Beat.*) Do you need a card?

Anne It's a rude one. That's what he's like. It's over there.

(*He gets it and passes it to her; she works.*)

I had a dream — it's the tritest, most pathetic dream I've ever had. I was water-skiing. Down the King's Road. Everyone was applauding. And suddenly you were behind me, riding in my wake, eating a baguette from Prêt à Manger, wearing bloomers. Orange bloomers. Everybody started laughing, and I thought I was going to die. So I grabbed you, pushed you into a shop and dressed you in the most divine olive-green Italian suit you've ever seen. Then we got back on our skis and everybody started applauding again.

Henry One ski or two?

Anne Henry ... It was very peculiar.

Henry So you want to be adored ...

Anne That's a sad, sad dream, a real indictment. Shows how shallow I can be, don't you think?

Henry You're not shallow.

Anne Some himbo stargazer at the theatre told me it meant that I was desperate to leave all of you behind.

Henry What do you mean, all of us?

Anne Everybody, all my friends. You included.

Henry What crap.

Anne Indeed.

(*Beat.*)

Henry We're just about to publish a book on dreams.

Anne I hate all that stuff.

Henry The print run's enormous. Trevor's buying one, of course.

Anne How typical. (*with the candlestick*) Ooops. This should be laid out in a box. Like me.

(*Beat.*)

Henry So ... you've seen him?

Anne (*busy*) You're very lovely together.

Henry Come off it, Anne.

Anne You are. Seriously. It works in public as well.

Henry What?

Anne Nothing. There's no need to be embarrassed, that's all.

Henry What the hell do you mean by that exactly?

Anne Embarrassed by him.

Henry (*cross*) I'm not.

Anne OK, good. As I say, you look good.

Henry I don't need your approval.

Anne Don't get mad with me. Sellotape, please. Three pieces.

Henry Here.

Anne Thank you, thanks, thanks. Ha. I couldn't do this on my own. I'm glad you were home when I called. (*works*) He talked about how he likes to sweat when he goes dancing. How he likes to shake his sweat. Sweat, it's one of his accoutrements. He said he liked dancing in a *sweat vacuum.* Ugh. Oh, Jesus, Frappy, what if it transfers?

Henry Then you'll be made.

Anne It's not quite like that, actually.

(*Beat.*)

Henry What would I know?

Anne (*looks at him*) Don't be cranky. I need you here.

(*She goes to him. Beat. She holds out the wrapped present.*)

How does this look?

Henry Mighty fine, Miss Scarlet.

Anne Why thank you. Ashley.

(*She works. Beat. She looks at her watch.*)

I'm running late. It's the morning! Would you mind wrapping that one? It'd be very helpful. It doesn't matter who the rest are for now. Could you?

Henry Of course.

Anne You're tremendous.

Henry Anne ...

Anne You are ... I'll do this one.

Henry Scissors.

Anne Here. (*suddenly*) Shit. (*looks at him*) Hell ... Am I going to be all right?

Henry I know it. You are. You will be wonderful. You are, always.

(**Anne** *smiles.*)

I can't wait. It'll be brilliant.

Anne (*mock scream*) Aaaahhhh! I want somebody to describe me as vital. I want to be a *vital* presence. Frappy!

(*She goes to him and kisses him on the lips. It lasts one second too long. She walks away. Smiles. Drinks. Eats.*)

More?

Henry No.

Anne (*suddenly*) It's your birthday soon, isn't it?

Henry Yes.

Anne What are we going to do?

Henry Whatever. You'll be in the middle of your season.

Anne Lunch.

Henry Don't worry about it.

Anne Just the two of us. We'll go somewhere really nice.
(*Beat.*)

Henry I'd love that.
(*Silence. They both wrap. As* **Henry** *works, he playfully sings a snatch of "Good Morning". Long pause.*)

Anne I don't know what that's from.

Henry What?

Anne I don't know what it's from.

Henry Don't you?

Anne No. I don't.
(*Beat.*)

Henry *Singin' in the Rain.*

Anne Oh. (*Beat. Still working.*) You're very camp, Henry.

Henry What? (*Beat.*) Don't say that. I am not.

Anne Yes you are. (*Beat.*) What's the matter?

Henry Bloody hell, Anne, I hate camp.

Anne Don't make me laugh. You drip it. (*Beat.*) I'm still hungry. I'll get something else. Let's have cheese and biccies.

Henry It's late ...

Anne Oh don't go. Please. I'm really on the edge here. Two days! Only one more preview! (*Beat*) Don't go yet.
(*Pause.*)

Henry All right. If that's what you want.

Anne Yes. How hungry are you?

Henry Starved actually.

(**Anne** *gets up. She touches him*)

I won't be a sec.

(*She kisses him on the forehead and goes out. Pause.* **Henry** *sighs, smiles, frowns, cups his nose and mouth with his hands for a moment, pauses, then continues wrapping. Crossfade.*)

Scene 12

A theatre foyer, Islington. The opening of **Anne**'s *play. The buzz of theatre-goers, etc.* **Henry** *looks smart, in a tie. He is reading the programme.* **Trevor** *enters, dressed up. He walks up to* **Henry**, *holding his hand out.*

Trevor Henry, great day, great evenin'!

Henry Hi, Trevor.

Trevor I'm glad I've made this. It was quite a journey, I can tell you, but I was early, I stopped off near the Angel for a quick bottle of Bud.

Henry Oh.

Trevor Not bad that place. Not very busy though.

Henry It's early.

Trevor Hen, Hen, Hen ... we're finally here. I can't wait for this, I can't wait.

Henry She'll be ... she'll be, pleased to see you.

Trevor Yeah, I saw 'er yesterday, and Sunday, come to that.

Henry Oh, really?

Trevor Yeah, she took me to Brighton, mate, never been before.

Henry Last Sunday?

Trevor Yeah.

Henry Two days ago?

Trevor We had a whale of a time — she showed me all the haunts you two used to go to.

Henry I can't remember our haunts. We haven't been to Brighton for a long time, I can't remember when.

Trevor (*looks around*) Wa'n't that long ago, she said — we did everythin', ate rock, walked out on the pier, dodgem-cars, bookshops, the lot!

Henry She didn't tell me.

Trevor Been busy, I expect. Have you seen 'er today?

Henry Yeah, before.

Trevor And? How's she feelin'? How's it all goin'?

Henry She's fine.

Trevor This is an important one, yeah?

Henry Yes, it is.

Trevor She told me she needs it to lead on to other things, like. I know 'ow she feels.

> (**Henry** *is uncomfortable, but smiles.* **Trevor** *smiles as well. Beat.*)

Caroline dragged me up here one day for some fund-raisin' thing, once, they were going to knock it down or somethin'. Actors and all sorts lyin' in front of the doors on the news and things.

> (*Beat.*)

Henry Come on, then, we'll get a drink.

Trevor Hey, hey, wait a mo. It was perfect! (*privately; intense*) Courtesy of Mr Roget I got ... (*uses his fingers to make quote signs in the air*) ... "baroque" and "florid" and "ornamented". And then it came to me, I decided to use your word in a different context. Get this, what d'ya reckon? (*pauses dramatically*) "Amy is the dominatrix, mark her magisterial frown / She is one of the most morally barren ..." I like that, I like that, came to me in a flash "morally barren", brilliant ... "In the whole of London town / Mark her ravishing torso / In her business it's the best / Lustrous, silky

66

white, with a pair of rococo breasts." Yeah? Imaginative? Thought so.

Henry Well done.

Trevor (*pleased as Punch*) Thanks, thanks a lot.

> (**Alec** *makes his way through the crowd.*)

Henry (*seeing him coming*) Oh, God. Here it comes.

Trevor What, mate ...?

Alec Excuse me, excuse me ... excuse me ... (*reaches them*) Hello, Henry. How nice to see you here! I knew you would be. Of course. (*holds out his hand*)

Henry (*shaking hands*) Hello, Alec.

Alec This is very exciting, is it not? Her first play in I don't know how long.

Henry Yes.

> (*Beat.*)

Alec I'm impressed by her commitment, Henry.

Henry She's been working hard.

Alec Yes. This is a significant opening night.

Henry Wouldn't have dreamed of missing it.

Alec (*smiling; looking at* **Trevor**) No.

> (*Uncomfortable pause.* **Alec** *still looks at* **Trevor**.)

(*to* **Henry**) I hear they've handled it like a banana.

Henry Excuse me?

Alec Peeled it. The skin, right off. To impart something fresh. Could be dated otherwise, I suppose. (*Beat.*) Anne's wearing salmon.

Henry I know.

> (*Beat.*)

Alec An ambiguous inquiry into the sex part, so I understand. Who is attracted to whom? Anne's lucky, they mightn't have cast the women at all.

(*Beat. He looks hard at* **Trevor** *and smiles.*)

A banana with the skin just ripped right off.

(*Beat.*)

Henry Oh, I'm sorry, this is Trevor. Trevor McCowan: Alec ... I'm sorry, I've forgotten your surname.

Alec Maybe you never knew it. Egon.

Henry Alec Egon.

Alec How do you do, Trevor, and are you Henry's friend or Anne's? (*holds out his hand*)

Trevor (*shaking hands*) Both of theirs.

Alec Both. Fascinating. I'll ask her about you.

Trevor Anne's the best.

Alec (*looking at them both; smiles*) I saw you both from afar. I wanted to come and have a chit-chat — there's nothing quite like a first night here, is there? But this isn't your side of London, is it? You don't live nearby, do you?

Henry No, miles from here.

Alec I thought so. The transport is satisfactory, I hope, across the river?

(*Beat.*)

Henry Anne seems happy with everything.

Alec Did it seem that way to you? I'm glad. I was: concerned myself. Mentally, she's still developing, adjusting herself to these new circumstances. But you're right, she'll cope. She's a good actress, Anne, very good indeed. I mean it too.

Trevor I helped 'er with 'er lines.

Alec You did? You can take some of the credit then, if she's any good.

Trevor Oh no, she'll be good, and it'll all be her doing.

Alec Would you like a drink, either of you?

(**Trevor** *is about to say yes.*)

Henry No thanks.

Alec (*looking around*) See her over there, the one so obviously on show, she's quite the young, bright, switched-on actress of the moment, isn't she, did you see her in the Stoppard?

Henry Oh. No.

Trevor She looks gaunt.

Henry Trevor ...

Trevor I like some flesh ...

Alec Yes, me too. You're quite right, she looks gaunt. Anorexic even. She's up in Stratford now ... We must try and get Anne some work with the RSC, what do you think?

Henry We must.

> (*Beat.*)

Alec Oh, look who I've seen. Sorry gentlemen, I have to fly ... We'll meet again soon, please.

Henry OK.

> (*Pause.*)

Alec (*looking at* **Henry**, *smiling*) I think you have a lot of untapped talent, Henry. Like Anne. (*Beat; to* **Trevor**) Goodbye.

Trevor Goodbye.

Alec (*to* **Henry**) Goodbye.

Henry Goodbye.

> (*They shake hands.* **Alec** *leaves.*)

Trevor What the hell?

> (**Henry** *is silent.*)

Who was that?

Henry He's a strange man.

Trevor You ain't kidding, weird science.

Henry I don't like him, I never have.

Trevor What's he got to do with Anne?

Henry Seemed like he owned her, didn't it?

Trevor You're not wrong.

　　　　(*Beat.*)

Henry That's the one, Trevor. He's the sugar daddy.

Trevor Oh, so that's what it was all about. God, where did she find 'im?

Henry Silly old queen.

Trevor No, I don't think so.

　　　　(**Henry** *looks at him. Beat.*)

(*looks off*) I know 'im — 'e's on TV.

　　　　(*Beat.*)

Henry (*checks his watch*) Do you want a drink, then?

Trevor Yeah.

Henry What?

Trevor Campari. Soda. Tall glass. Ice and a slice.

　　　　(**Henry** *looks at him, then gets the drinks.*)

I 'aven't been this excited in a long while. (*Beat.*) I wonder how she is? (*Beat.*) Hen. What's she doing now?

Henry Who?

Trevor Anne.

Henry She's in her dressing-room, I suppose ...

Trevor Right ...

Henry Well not *her* dressing-room, I don't think this theatre's up to that ...

Trevor That'd be it. Doing her make-up. When I was in the theatre I was always slapping on number nine!

Henry Me too dahrling!

　　　　(*Beat.*)

Trevor She never normally wears much make-up, does she? I noticed.

Henry Don't think she needs to.

Trevor Nah, I don't suppose she does ... she 'as perfect skin.

70

(*Pause.*)

Henry (*lyrical*) In her dressing-room, doing her make-up, *applying* her make-up; calm, but occupied, drinking from a bottle of Evian, dabbing her face with a powder-puff, maybe having a drag or two on someone else's cigarette.

Trevor Typical!

(*Beat.* **Henry** *looks off.*)

Busy, i'n't it?

Henry Yeah.

Trevor Anne said it would be like this. Sticky. (*Pause. He looks around.*) What now?

Henry What?

Trevor Anne.

Henry Anne ... Well ... now she finishes her make-up and flicks at her eyelashes and swirls her tongue behind her lips. And she ignores everyone, everyone, everyone, and puts her headphones on and listens to Glenn Gould, turning the Preludes and Fugues up very loud ...

Trevor Bach ...

Henry Yeah ... so that she can hear nothing else but the music.

Trevor She ignores everyone ...

Henry ... and she sits silently on a wooden chair in the wings long before she is called, confident it's going to be a hit. She stretches her arms up high above her head and smiles, breathes heavily and thinks of ... of ...

Trevor Us. (*triumphant*) She thinks of us!

(*Beat.* **Trevor** *smiles and holds his glass up.* **Henry** *looks at him.*)

(*Blackout. Music.*)

(*Interval here if required.*)

71

Scene 13

Henry's *flat, late evening. His birthday.* **Henry**, **Anne** *and* **Trevor**, *sitting. They are drinking.* **Henry** *has bottled beer.* **Anne** *is flicking through a magazine. Pause.* **Henry** *drinks.* **Trevor** *looks at* **Anne** *briefly, then looks at* **Henry**, *then smiles, then drinks. Pause.*

Anne (*after a while, sluggish*) This is the sort of rag that Henry gets, Trevor.

Trevor Very glossy ...

Anne It's an opera magazine, look. Sometimes they have some excellent articles on ...

　　(*She pauses, flicking through the pages, flirtatiously.*)

Henry Opera?

Anne Yes. Opera.

Trevor I read the poetry magazines myself.

Anne Do you?

Trevor Yeah.

　　(*Silence.*)

Anne (*to* **Henry**) Where's Martin?

Henry Out with Sally.

Trevor Or whatever 'er name is.

Anne Did they celebrate with you?

Henry No.

Trevor Oh, pity.

Henry We're not that close.

Anne It's just us then.

Henry Yes. (*Beat.*) The day's almost over, anyway.

Trevor Can't 'elp that though, can we? Anne here has these odd hours, she's got the London literati to keep 'appy now. Haven't you?

(**Anne** *smiles at him. Beat, uncomfortable.*)

And 'appy they are. (*smiles, pauses, drinks*) Hate flatmates, me. (*Pause.*) Another one bites the dust then, Henry?

Henry I suppose.

Trevor We're all getting older, eh? That's the one constant in life. God, we'll all be thirty soon. Come-on-Eileen, imagine that.

(*Beat.*)

Anne (*puts magazine down*) I'm sorry I couldn't come for lunch. Really.

Henry How was it this evening?

Anne Extremely good, the whole thing is such a buzz.

Trevor Yeah. Superb. Groundbreaking, I'd say.

(*Silence.* **Trevor** *laughs a little and toasts the air. He drinks.*)

Henry More?

Trevor Nah, still going on this.

Henry Anne?

(*Beat.*)

Anne I've had way too much to drink lately. It feels like I've been drinking hour after hour for days. Every night, we all go out afterwards. It's too much. (*Beat.*) I'll say it myself, I've been getting lots of praise.

Trevor You deserve it, you're a star.

(**Henry** *looks annoyed.* **Anne** *smiles.*)

Like a real star, you are, like W. Ryder, I'm telling you.

(*Pause.*)

Anne He's seen it three times, Frappy.

Henry I know.

Trevor Four including tonight.

Anne Four times!

Trevor They know me there now; I always get the best

seats. (*to* **Anne**) Caroline was saying today she thought you were terrif.

Henry Caroline?

Trevor Yeah. (*Beat.*) Entre nous, I've gone off Caroline a bit lately. She was sniffy that I knew someone in *Who's Afraid of Virginia Woolf?* (*looks at* **Anne**) ... Well, it's the hit of the season, this, i'n't it, Hen? Still, I rose above it. The broccoli at the Safeways on the Edgware Road: I was very gallant when she dropped the shopping.

Anne Gallant?

Trevor Yeah, gallant. No one in Paddington as gallant as I. That's right, i'n't it, Hen?

Henry I hadn't thought about it.

Trevor Well there's you of course, when you're over my way. (*to* **Anne**) Whizzer with the ladies.

(*Beat.*)

Henry I ...

Anne Yes?

Henry I saw the reviews.

Anne Uhuh.

Henry Yours were very favourable.

Anne I like that. Very favourable. They were mind-boggling, Frappy. I couldn't have hoped for better.

(*Pause. They drink.*)

Trevor (*suddenly*) Oh, shit me! I forgot to get you a present.

Henry It doesn't matter.

Trevor It does. I can't believe it ... I forgot to get him a present.

Henry I don't ... make a big deal about ... birthdays.

Trevor Damn ... Wait! I might have something in me bag ...

Henry Trevor, forget it.

Trevor I'll get you something.

Henry Don't worry.

Trevor No, I will ... I'll get you a book or something. Hey, you got a copy of Anne's play?

Henry Somewhere.

Trevor I 'aven't seen it on your bookshelf. That's what I'll get for ya! It's only a paperback, but you've gotta have that one. You can't not have *that*. I'll get it for you. It's a Penguin paperback. (*Beat.*) Anne has a copy that's signed and everything.

    (*Beat. They drink.*)

Damn, what's a birthday party without presents? (*Beat.*) Or the video of the film with the lovely Liz T. Yeah.

    (*Beat.*)

Henry It's not a birthday party.

    (*Beat. They drink.*)

Why wasn't Alec at the cast party, afterwards?

Anne Who?

Henry Alec. He was at the theatre, at the opening: we saw him in the foyer. Why didn't we see him afterwards?

    (*Beat.*)

He came bursting through the crowd talking about you as if he was your agent or something, didn't he Trevor?

Trevor (*after hesitating*) He was that protective of you, yeah.

Anne Why do you take any notice of the man? Don't.

Henry It's strange ... why wasn't he at the party?

Anne I can't remember anything about that night — it's all a fantastic blur. (*drinks*) I'm not seeing him a lot any more.

Henry No need I suppose, now that you're working ... and earning.

    (**Anne** shoots **Henry** *a look. Pause.*)

Anne Trevor, Frappy was all set to live with me once.

Trevor Were you, Hen? I didn't know that.

Anne But he chose this place, what do you think?

Trevor I'd've chosen you.

Henry It suits me fine this way.

Anne I don't think so. Underneath it all, you need looking after.

Henry I don't.

Trevor He does! I look after 'im, for starters!

Henry Trevor ...

Trevor He can't cook anythin', can he?

(*Pause.*)

Henry (*patiently*) Once, Trevor brought over a curry.

Trevor I cooked it from a recipe left by this friend of mine, a student from Malaysia — no good for anythin' but the curry, mind. I brought everythin' over on the tube, didn't I, Hen? Tray, curry in an oven-dish wrapped in foil, plate, knife and fork, glass and a bottle of XD.

Anne Why?

Trevor Just to make it a complete caterin' service. Got some strange looks on the tube. It was worth it though, it's a fab curry, the best. I'll make some for you if you like.

Anne Why not!

Trevor It's hot stuff —

Henry (*interrupting*) It's the only time you've ever cooked for me; you're hardly meals-on-wheels.

Trevor Well, I'd love to do it again. Any time. You just give me an 'oy. There is nothing like this Malaysian curry.

Anne Really?

Trevor Straight from Kuala Lumpur! Bellissimo!

(**Henry** *looks at* **Anne**. *She laughs. Silence.*)

Actually, we could do with some nosh now.

Henry I don't have anything.

Trevor What's a birthday party without food?

Henry It's not a birthday *party*. (*Pause.*) It's just my birthday.

Trevor We could call out for pizza, do you want that?

Anne Yuk.

Trevor Maybe not.

Anne (*suddenly*) Oh, speaking of opera ...

Henry What?

Anne I forgot to ask you, Trevor ... damn. What are you doing tomorrow afternoon?

Trevor Working, I got an extra shift. Why?

Anne Oh ... I meant to say something to you before ... I have a ticket to the Coliseum, you could have come. I would have loved to have known what you thought. Lesley Garrett in rehearsal.

Trevor Oh, I love her.

    (*Beat.*)

Henry Do you?

Trevor Very down-to-earth.

Anne (*smiling, impressed*) She is.

Trevor Yeah.

Anne (*avoiding* **Henry**) It's some dire French operetta they've set in the roaring forties, but it would have been fun.

Trevor Damn. Shame.

Henry (*to* **Anne**, *sombre*) *La Vie Parisienne.*

Trevor What was that?

Henry Nothing.

    (*Beat.* **Henry** *looks at* **Anne**, *hard. She drinks.*)

Anne Call me if you can change your shift. (*finishes her drink*) What about Sunday, are you free then?

Trevor Yeah. (*clocking* **Henry**) Are you free on Sunday, Henry?

Henry I don't know.

Trevor We could all go out, Sunday. All three of us if you like. Yeah?

Anne Yes.

Trevor Henry?

Anne Let's.

Trevor Henry?

Anne Oh, come on, why not, all of us. That's better. It'll be fun ...

Henry Fine.

Anne Well don't look so down about it. (*Pause*) Trevor, arrange it through me.

(*Beat. She looks at her watch.*)

(*to* **Henry**) Sorry. It's getting a bit late for me now.

Trevor I should get going myself.

Anne Oh.

(*Beat.*)

Trevor You going out, mate? Early days, yet. Especially round 'ere.

Henry A quiet night in, that's all. Bed, in fact.

Trevor Oh well, don't let it get you down.

(*Beat.*)

(*to* **Anne**) We could catch a minicab back north together.

Anne Yes. It's on the way. We'll do that. Good.

(*Beat.*)

Trevor I'll get you that birthday present mate, don't you worry.

(**Anne** *turns her face away and smiles in spite of herself.*)

Henry What's so funny?

Anne Nothing. (*Pause. She toasts him.*) Many happy returns.

Trevor Said Shirley Maclaine to her guru. (*toasts*)

(*Pause. Music. Crossfade.*)

Scene 14

Trevor's *flat.* **Henry** *and* **Trevor**. **Trevor** *drinks beer. He is working on a model aeroplane.*

Trevor What do you think of this? It's a World War Two bomber.

Henry Yeah.

Trevor Rent payment's going up.

Henry Is it?

Trevor Bugger, i'n't it?

Henry Certainly is.

Trevor I'll put some music on.

Henry Fine.

　　　(**Trevor** *puts some music on. Trashy pop blares.*)

Turn it down a bit.

Trevor Yeah, we can't 'ear ourselves think, can we? (*turns it down*) I'm going through a phase. (*finishes model*) There. Don't s'pose you really go in for this stuff.

Henry In small measures.

Trevor Hey! It's better than all that Philip Glass shit you 'ave over your place.

Henry I told you, Anne gave them to me.

Trevor Ah yes. Anne.

　　　(*He reaches for his beer and nearly knocks over the model*)

Henry Watch it!

Trevor It's just a hobby, Hen, nothin' important. Hey, do you want to hear my latest poem?

Henry Of course.

Trevor It's imprudent of me to show you. Imprudent. Good word that. I saw it the other day. In some novel.

(*He swigs some beer and slams it down; he knocks the model and it goes careering to the floor.*)

Oh, bugger.

Henry Here, let me ...

Trevor Forget it, it's cheap shit anyway.

(*There is a knock on the door.*)

Who's that? Damn. Hold on.

(*He goes out to get the door.*)

(*off*) Caroline!

Caroline (*off*) Hi, Trevor.

Trevor (*off*) Come in.

Caroline (*off*) No, I only came to get that —

(**Trevor** *enters, ushering in* **Caroline**.)

Trevor Look who's here: Caroline.

Henry Hi, Caroline.

Caroline Hello. (*Pause.*) Look: Trevor —

Trevor (*interrupts*) Hey! You can listen to it too. It's that ready, I'm telling you.

Caroline What?

Trevor The latest poem.

Caroline Trevor, I just came to get the book.

Trevor Yeah, I've got it. Here, sit down.

Caroline No, I can't stay ...

Trevor Please ...

Caroline All right, briefly.

Henry How are you?

Caroline I'm fine. Thank you.

Trevor I've just got to get it. Hold on. (*as he goes*) Get a drink, why don't you, Caroline — plenty in the fridge.

(*He exits. Pause.*)

Caroline (*sitting*) So how is it with you and your friend Trevor? He's been very busy lately, if my dear old aunt's lorgnette is anything to go by.

Henry He's not my friend Trevor.

Caroline He tried to ask me out the other day.

Henry I know.

Caroline (*without malice*) There have to be restrictions in my life now, and he is way, way on the wrong side of the double yellow line.

Henry Why do you lend him books?

Caroline (*smiling*) He doesn't so much borrow them as steal them. You're cute, really, you are. (*Beat.*) What's taking him so long?

Henry (*calling*) Trevor.

Trevor (*off*) Hold on! Adjustments!

Caroline Have you noticed how he leers all the time?

Henry I know.

Caroline The first time I met him, when he moved in here, too long ago, he leered.

Henry He leered when I met him, too.

Caroline Do you like him?

Henry He's a show-off.

(*Pause.*)

Caroline He walks down the front there sometimes, on his way to the gym, or wherever it is that he gets to, springing on his toes, and his arse sticks up in the air, high and inviting ... virile. He crosses the road, all postured, with his arms away from his torso ...

Henry He's a show-off.

Caroline ... sometimes I'm absolutely disgusted and other times I'm so turned on I could die. (*Pause.*) Once — before I made him out of bounds — we went out, I can't remember what for, miles and miles, East, and this man came up to us and asked us where a Turkish sauna was. And Trevor knew. "It's a tenner to get in," he said.

Henry Strange.

Caroline It's all in the poetry, everything you want to know.

Henry (*surprised*) You've read it before this?

Caroline Some.

Henry The stuff about you?

Caroline It's not about me ... *specifically*. Just my friends. He hates my friends.

Henry Yes.

Caroline It's terrible, isn't it?

Henry Atrocious.

(**Trevor** *enters.*)

Trevor Sorry, I discovered there were one or two last minute changes ...

Caroline Never mind.

Trevor Hen, I forgot to tell you: my parents are comin'.

Henry From Dorset?

Trevor Yep.

Caroline This should be fun.

Henry Are they staying with you?

Trevor Oh, no, couldn't 'ave that — they're goin' round the corner to one of those bed breakfast places. Henry, they want to meet you.

Henry Me?

Trevor Yeah. Well, not just you ... they want to meet some of my friends. But you they 'ave to meet. With a friend like you I can show them I'm gettin' somewhere with the poetry.

Caroline Oh, please.

Henry Why? What do you mean?

Trevor Well, you're the wordsmith, aren't you, you've been

82

to university and you're in publishing and all that ... they'll see I'm getting somewhere. Yeah. So, come over and see them.

Henry Er, when?

Trevor Few weeks.

Henry OK ... thank you ... that will be ... nice.

Trevor Mum's cooking. This is brill.

Caroline Simply brill.

Trevor (*turns off the music*) OK, everybody. Ready?

Caroline Ready.

Trevor (*standing, declaiming dramatically*) "I'm in love with Soho: with Frith Street / With the smelly and dark 'Fast Bar' / Where, every night, the shades are down / And there's the smell of incense all around ... / I'm in love with Alice Hollowbrook / Who comes into the room, snarling / 'I've just done a show, darling!'" ... that's a messy rhyme there, I'll fix that rhyme ... "I'm in love with her voice as it barks / In the dark / Its tone as sharp / As the teeth of a shark ..." I like that bit.

Caroline The wonders of a rhyming dictionary.

Trevor Hey! How did you know? I couldn't do without it.

Caroline Do you know what a malapropism is?

Trevor Sure. Anyway ... (*continues*) "As rough as tree bark / I'm in love with Alice / She of the 'Fast Bar'" (*with frenzied passion*) "I'll buy her a fast car / To take her away, I will by gaddy / From her life of artifice and loneliness / And her evil Sugar Daddy."

(*Pause.*)

Caroline Well. What's it all about?

Henry Trevor, I don't think you can do that.

Trevor What?

Henry I know what that's about ... I know who that is ...

Trevor You do as a matter of fact. Remember that prozzie we

83

saw down the road after we first met? It's 'er. I've given 'er an 'istory, turned her into a second-rate actress, relocated 'er to Soho. Clever, huh?

Caroline Her name is Alice!

Trevor Yeah, d'ya like it? It gives it a bit of a, sort of, Lewis Carroll flavour. Bit Wonderlandy.

Henry It seems ... a bit close to the bone, actually.

Trevor What do you mean?

Henry You're not ... what's all that stuff about ...?

 (*Pause.*)

Trevor What.

Henry (*firmly*) Have you spoken to Anne lately, Trevor?

Trevor Of course I 'ave, all the time, mate.

Henry It's not Anne you've relocated to Soho, by any chance, is it?

Trevor Knock it off, mate.

Henry You know: you can't. Do that. She's not one of your cheap ...

Trevor What? (*Pause.*) It's out of my hands, this, it's poetry, I use everybody for that. Everybody.

Henry Well you can't use Anne.

Trevor I'm not using Anne, I haven't. (*Beat.*) You don't like it.

Henry I didn't say that.

Trevor Why can't I write about whatever I like, anyway? She's not yours.

Henry No ... she's not.

 (*Beat.*)

Caroline Trevor, do you think I could get the book, and then I'll leave. (*Pause.*) For what it's worth, I enjoyed it.

Henry (*quickly*) Yes, it's a beauty, Trevor. I'm sorry, though, I have to go, really, I have to go. (*gets up*) Bye, Caroline.

Caroline Bye-bye.

Henry Bye, Trevor.

Trevor Bye, Hen. I'll write some new stuff, I'll make it a bit less contentious, hey? But you've gotta take the bull by the horns, yeah, if you want to write poetry.

Henry Yeah.

Trevor Cheers, then.

Henry Bye.

Trevor Oy! Hen. Don't forget about my parents. In a few weeks. I'll let you know.

Henry Fine.

Trevor Ciao!

> (**Henry** *looks back at* **Trevor**. *Music. Crossfade.*)

Scene 15

Trevor's *flat.* **Henry**, **Anne** *and* **Trevor**, *after a dinner party with* **Trevor**'s *parents. They are all a bit drunk.*

Trevor (*calling at the door*) Bye! Bye-bye! Yes ... Mum, all right!! (*pokes his head back into the room*) I better see them down to the cab.

> (*He exits.*)

Henry (*to himself*) Don't leave your heterosexual friends up there for too long, Trevor.

Anne (*arch*) Interesting.

> (*Beat.*)

Henry He even writes poetry about you, now.

Anne Yes I know that.

Henry I heard one. It's a pitiful *roman-à-clef*. You work in Frith Street in something called the "Fast Bar".

Anne That's old, Frappy. There have been many since then.

Henry He makes you cheap.

    (*Beat.*)

Anne I've never had anyone write poetry about me before.

Henry That's pathetic.

Anne Fuck off, Frappy, I haven't. (*Pause.*) He's desperate to sleep with me. (*Beat.*) I haven't allowed it to happen. Yet.

    (*She smiles.* **Henry** *looks at her.*)

But he likes men too.

Henry Yes ... well ... not according to his parents.

Anne You've slept with him, naturally?

    (*Pause.*)

Henry Not exactly.

Anne Of course you have.

Henry No, really, not exactly. Yes I have. But ... well, not ...

Anne Not penetration?

Henry Well ... no ... not really.

Anne I don't know what that means: "Well ... no ... not really." I suppose it's all perverse and messed-up for you isn't it?

Henry What?

Anne Your sort.

Henry (*very shocked*) Anne!

    (*Beat.*)

Anne I'm sorry. I didn't meant that. (*Beat.*) It's all over him, he *loves* men.

Henry I can tell you he brings plenty of women home as well. And there's Caroline, upstairs. He's in love with her.

Anne Other men too?

Henry Yes.

Anne Aside from you. (*Pause.*) Yes. As I thought.

Henry Anne. You should ... you should keep your wits about you.

(**Trevor** *enters.*)

Anne (*mocking*) "We did well to bring him into this world."

Trevor (*brightly*) Get away.

Anne They're lovely people, Trev, so nice and friendly. It's sweet — you walk just like your dad.

Trevor They both loved you.

Anne Oh, good! I am glad.

Trevor And you too, Hen, they thought you were capital.

Anne The food was wonderful.

Trevor She did it all for you. She's not a bad cuisine-maker, my mum. (*looks at* **Anne**) Make yourself comfy, Anne, I've gotta pop to the men's room. Back in a mo.

     (**Trevor** *exits. Long pause.*)

Henry You were obviously a hit.

Anne Yes, I was.

     (*Beat.*)

Henry I haven't seen you for ages.

Anne No, Frappy darling, it's been a while.

Henry How's Alec?

Anne Why?

Henry I didn't know you were going to be here tonight.

Anne I was only invited this afternoon.

Henry Really?

Anne Trevor thought he'd make it a real party.

Henry Well, for that we need you.

     (*Pause.*)

Anne Do you like my fingernails?

Henry Yes. You keep them well.

Anne My long, spidery, fingernails, unpolished for a Saturday. Poor fingernails. (*Pause.*) It was exciting having no idea where that wine came from.

87

Henry Anne ...

Anne No. It's exciting. It could have been from *anywhere*. It could've been from Newcastle. (*Pause; quietly*) You have a problem, don't you?

Henry Have you been seeing him?

Anne You know I have.

Henry "Yes, Mrs McCowan," you were saying ...

Anne What ...?

Henry You were saying it ... your whole body was saying it, the way you went on about your ... everything ... your career: you do *not* know Bruce Forsyth. (*Beat.*) "Yes, Mrs McCowan. I'm with Trevor. We have a future together. We are going to get married, I'm going to stop him writing lewd poetry and I am going to have your grandchildren ..."

Anne Oh ... you ... that's disgusting ... you're disgusting.

Henry No, you're disgusting. I've never seen such a performance. You should try acting. (*Pause.*) Neither of you give two hoots for each other, really.

Anne He's a pillock.

(*Pause.*)

Henry Do you know what's amazing? Look at this place: there's been no censorship. For their visit. (*pointing to posters on the walls*) *Taxi Driver*, fine, Kim Basinger with her tits out, fine, but look, through there, his bedroom door wide open so that all and sundry can see a huge blow-up of Moana de la Miner — of the Vauxhall Tavern de la Miners? Never heard of her? She's the regular eleven p.m. act there every Friday night, a lip-synching Minnelli wannabe. It's so corny, Anne. Liza with an E. God how I hate gay anthems. Vauxhall, Anne, have you ever even *been* to dank, dingy Vauxhall? (*Beat.*) In case you didn't know, she is one of Trevor's good friends. And there she is above his bed, with red sequins and stubble, trying to look impish. It's pretty obvious if you've got half a brain that she's a bloke. But do the parentals, Mr and Mrs thick-woollen-jumper-McCowan, even think to ask questions? Why should they? Thanks to your behaviour and his obscene lies it's much nicer, much more convenient to presume that you two are going steady ... that you will become their sodding daughter-in-law.

Anne I'm not going to listen ... to ... *this*.

    (**Trevor** *enters.*)

Oh, good. My turn.

Trevor Right you are. Actually, get me some floss while you're in there wouldja? Mum's meals are a bit stringy between the teeth.

    (**Anne** *exits.*)

Anne (*off*) Oh, Trevor how too divine, I hadn't noticed. Marilyn Monroe on your shower curtain. And it's like a hologram!

Henry There's a joke there somewhere about a seven year itch.

Trevor Yeah. (*Pause.*) Thanks for everything. The evening was a poem.

Henry Could I have another drink?

Trevor (*over this*) You'll leave now, won't you?

Henry Pardon?

Trevor (*charmingly*) Thanks for coming around. But I think you might like to go now though, if you know what I mean.

Henry Um, no.

Trevor Great friends, the greatest.

Henry Right.

Trevor I feel it now, though, Hen. The time is right, you know? You wouldn't want to spoil my plum, wouldja, mate?

Henry What?

Trevor Spoil my plum.

Henry Oh, oh, no ... no ...

Trevor You know how it is.

(**Henry** *guffaws wryly and gets up, slowly, to get his coat.*)

Trevor Do y'wanna cab?

Henry No. Thank you. I'll walk for a while.

Trevor Still early.

Henry Yes. Very. Always.

Trevor Never know what might be out there. (*Pause.*) It was the best, this evening.

(*Pause.* **Henry** *looks hard at* **Trevor**.)

Henry I can't believe this ...

Trevor I'll be in touch.

(*He smiles. Beat.*)

Henry (*calls*) Goodnight, Anne. (*Pause.*) Goodnight, Anne.

Anne (*off*) Goodnight, Frappy darling. See you soon. We should do lunch, some time. (*Beat.*) Hold on.

(*She enters.*)

Bye, Frappy. (*kisses him*)

Trevor (*offering his hand*) Bye, wordsmith.

Henry Bye.

(*He half moves to peck* **Trevor** *on the cheek.* **Trevor** *puts his hand on* **Henry**'s *shoulder.*)

Trevor See ya.

Henry Thanks, Trevor.

Trevor Thank you. Rococo. Great word.

(*He punches* **Henry** *on the arm and whisks him towards the door. Music, something chart-busting, poppy. Lights begin to fade as* **Henry** *walks slowly out, then turns to look. Music louder, as* **Anne** *and* **Trevor** *embrace and lower themselves to the ground, kissing passionately. Lights fade to a single spot on* **Henry**, *who looks at them, mortified. The music gets very loud. Crossfade.*)

Scene 16

Alec's *London flat, Holland Park*. **Henry** *and* **Alec**. **Henry** *is sitting*.

Alec Why are you here?

Henry Because I didn't know, all the time I've known you, what you really are to Anne and I feel sick, betrayed about that.

Alec There's no need. It isn't relevant. Why now?

Henry I want you to keep away from her.

Alec How melodramatic of you.

(*Beat.*)

Henry A couple of months ago we were watching *The Magnificent Ambersons* at the Everyman Cinema in Hampstead.

Alec Ah, yes. One of her favourites, I recall.

Henry We've watched it together a few times. She was in good form. We had lots of giggles about Agnes Moorehead. "All that spite!" Anne kept saying, "All that hysteria! Madly over the top! Oooh, Frappy, I can't wait to see her again! Dear Agnes!" (*Beat.*) But my head just throbbed, Alec. All I could do was think of you. Halfway through the film I was ... repelled by Anne's merriment, the cinema seemed ridiculous, Agnes Moorehead was tedious, and I found it hard to believe that I was ever taken in by that actressy turn of hers.

Alec What was the problem? Henry.

Henry It suddenly occurred to me that ... that ...

Alec Yes?

Henry That you'd ... abused her.

(*Beat.*)

Alec (*brightly*) I've always considered myself a bit of a cross-generationalist. My good friends are my good friends' chil-

91

dren. (*Beat.*) When Anne was five, she asked her mother —
she-what-was-done-in-by-too-much-gin — what DNA was!
That slip-up convinced she-what-was-done-in-by-too-much-gin
that she had a prodigy, a child-genius, on her hands. But it
came to pass that Anne was decidedly average. (*Beat.*) Did
you know that I bought most of the furniture in Anne's
house? I suppose you gathered that. A lot of restoration was
done on that Georgian mahogany sideboard in the hall. *That*
cost me a fortune. (*Beat; soft, grave*) You think she's *yours*,
don't you?

Henry Pardon me?

Alec You like strutting about with her, don't you?

Henry I know she doesn't need me any more, never did.

Alec We are all vile little men, you know. All men are vile. I
think you understand me, don't you. Think of all the things
you've done. They're vile, aren't they? Do you think she's
yours?

Henry No.

Alec Good.

Henry I'm sorry, Alec. I shouldn't be here.

Alec You don't know why you're here, do you?

Henry I've been worried. I'm just so worried.

Alec You feel like she's been unfaithful, Henry?

Henry What?

Alec Because she fucked your boyfriend?

    (*Beat.*)

Henry He's not my boyf —

Alec No. And I'm not your therapist. So.

    (*Beat.*)

Henry All along I've wanted to say — it's just that she has
to be ... well, she has to be careful with Trevor. Safe.

Alec No more careful than she needs to be with anybody.

Henry No, maybe not.

Alec Stop kidding me around, Henry.

Henry He's a lout you know. He writes bad, bad poetry and he comes all the way to Clapham just to show it off and I'm too kind to tell him the truth. It's pretentious and shallow. And he has sex with more people than I know. He doesn't care who they are, he just goes out and picks them up from these seedy places he goes to. He spends half his time in front of the mirror, and he listens to rotten music and well, Jesus Alec, he's just a bloody drip.

Alec But you like him a lot, don't you?

Henry Yes.

Alec Your visit here is pointless. (*Beat.*) She knows what she's doing, let her be.

Henry Did you do that to her?

Alec What?

Henry Why don't I know? Anything. Did you abuse her?

    (*Beat.* **Alec** *starts laughing.*)

Alec You're serious, aren't you?

Henry I just want ... information. Anything ... please ...

Alec Yes. You're brave to ask me. Something. That's impressive. You don't ask enough questions, Henry, I've noticed. You don't *do* enough. You think you're on the watch but you never *see*. See? Scrutinize, Henry. (*Pause.*) I have never abused her, she has never been made to do anything she didn't want to do. In the end our relationship, such that it was, was all about dosh.

Henry You can stop doing that now — you can stop giving her money.

Alec Oh, give it up. It is a long time since you've seen her. (*Beat.*) It's already been arranged that I stop, Henry. She's done it herself.

    (*Pause.* **Alec** *smiles and reaches into his jacket.* **Henry** *reacts a little fearfully.*)

(*as charming as can be*) Here is my card.

Henry Pardon me?

Alec (*still holding the card out*) This is my card, Henry, with my New York number. I'm going back for a while. To my apartment, you should see it. On the Upper West Side. It's surrounded by actors and writers and painters. You'd fit in very well.

Henry Why would I want your number? Put it away.

Alec My secretary will put you through to me, when I'm there. For whenever you want to talk.

Henry I won't ever want to talk to you.

Alec One day, when Anne — she-what-drinks-too-much-gin, mark two — has disappeared off the face of the earth, just like her parents did, or, if fate plays a different hand, and she becomes so famous that you won't be worth the dirt that her Sloaney feet tread upon, you may want a piece of her. And I am giving you my address so that you can come and talk to me. I know more about that girl than you'll ever know. Come see me. Sometime. We'll share memories. And I'll have more than you. Here's my card.

Henry I don't know whether you're some twisted, fucked-up sicko or not.

Alec You make me want to retch, Henry, certainly. Don't you ever come here unannounced again — no more of these mysterioso arrivals, all right? I don't like them. (*smiling*) Call me first.

> (*Beat. He stuffs the card into* **Henry**'s *shirt pocket and holds out his hand.*)

Goodbye, Henry. Take care.

Henry I really want to hurt you.

> (*Long pause.* **Alec** *smiles. Suddenly,* **Henry** *punches* **Alec***, an almighty wallop in the stomach that makes him double-over and cry out in pain.* **Henry** *stares at him. Crossfade.*)

Scene 17

Near **Trevor's** *flat, late at night.* **Henry** *loiters, waiting.* **Trevor** *enters; he seems drunk. He sings a line of "I Wouldn't Normally Do This Kind of Thing".*

Henry Trevor ...?

(**Trevor** *sees* **Henry** *and sobers in an instant.*)

Trevor Henry, mate.

Henry (*smiles*) Hi.

Trevor Look at you out this hour, and all on your own.

Henry Sorry, it's a bit late, I shouldn't have ... I thought you were upstairs. The light's on.

Trevor Oh, right. No, I 'ad to whip down to that Indian twenty-four hour joint for a few vitals. (*He looks up to his window.*) Um ... Hen. Yeah. It's been too long. (*Beat.*) I was reading a grippin' article in the *Independent*, that *is* my chosen organ, yesterday, all about the diminishin' interest in London as the settin' for contemporary novels. Didja see it?

Henry No, I didn't I'm afraid. Look ... I don't want to interrupt anything, Trevor, just passing.

Trevor Just passin' through Paddington, eh, aren't they all? (*Beat.*) Very erudite it was, this piece. I showed it to Caroline who ignored it with an 'uff, but it's true you know, the place doesn't universally pulsate, does it ...? You know, like New York *pulsates* ... (*Pause; softly*) Henry, mate ...

Henry I'll get going.

Trevor Did you come 'ere to see me?

Henry Um ...

Trevor You should have rung, yeah? I'm sorry, I've got Andromeda up there tonight.

Henry Mm. I'll go. Sorry, Trevor ...

Trevor (*quickly*) No, no, don't go. (*Beat.*) Look, look, stay a bit. Sit. It's all right, I'm not going to talk to you all night about the decline of the London novel, am I?

Henry Well ...

Trevor Got something I wanna show you 'ere, anyway. It's a new poem.

Henry Oh.

Trevor It's about you, actually.

Henry Is it?

Trevor Don't panic. I 'ad this ... this picture in my head, and I just 'ad to get it out. It's really weird. I reckon you're a muse or something. I've been writing some great stuff since I've known you — this is one of me best.

Henry How strange.

Trevor It's just a matter of time before I'm published now, I reckon.

Henry That's what your mum and dad think, anyway.

Trevor Sure, sure. (*grabs some crumpled paper out of his back pocket*) Take this, read it wouldja? Let me know whatcha think.

Henry OK, I will.

Trevor I really want your opinion, you know, your advice. Let me know ... read it soon ...

Henry I will. Thanks. (*puts the paper in his pocket*)

Trevor No, no, thank *you* ... wordsmith.

(**Henry** *smiles. They sit back and look at the sky.*)

Henry Nice night.

Trevor Bit cold.

Henry There have been so many calm nights lately. I walk around all the time now, at night.

Trevor Yeah.

(*Pause.* **Trevor** *lights a cigarette.*)

Drag?

Henry Thanks.

> (*He has a drag then hands the cigarette back to* **Trevor**.)

Trevor Yeah, yep, yep, yep, yep, yep.

> (*Long pause.*)

Henry So, how's Caroline?

Trevor Huh? Ah, she's preparing for an exhibition at that stupid art gallery in Notting Hill.

Henry I haven't been there for a while.

Trevor She'll never be ready, you know.

Henry Why not?

Trevor She has, like, plaster everywhere.

Henry What's new?

Trevor This is worse. She's workin' on four or five things at once.

Henry What is it? A series?

Trevor Somethin' like that. Somethin' to do with women's insides — creation or procreation or menstruation or something. I can't see it though. She won't let me 'ave a look.

Henry Well, I suppose she's flat-out.

Trevor Yeah, always too busy with that bloody gallery. (*Pause.*) She doesn't give a shit for me, anyway.

Henry She does like you, I think.

Trevor She's a cow.

Henry Yeah.

Trevor (*laughs*) Yeah.

> (*Pause.* **Trevor** *smokes. They both look upwards.*)

Henry That's the fattest cat I've seen in Paddington, **Trevor**. You've been feeding that one, haven't you?

Trevor Rotten thing. (*Pause.*) I 'aven't seen Anne, you know, not for a long time.

> (**Henry** *looks at him.*)

She's great, right, I like her, but she's gotta few problems, that one; latched 'erself on to me for a bit, then she was gone. I feel a bit rotten about it, left you for dead.

(*Pause.*)

Henry It's all right.

Trevor Yep, she annihilates reality, that one.

Henry Excuse me?

Trevor She annihilates reality.

Henry Where did you read that?

Trevor Fuck off.

(*Pause.*)

Henry Sorry. (*Beat.*) We all deny things, if that's what you're talking about.

Trevor That's what I *am* talkin' about. She does it all the time, you noticed? She either gets on stage, or she walks tall with you or she drinks too much gin and tonic and snorts god-knows-what or she criticizes everyone around her, or she goes all King's Roady or she has sex — all these things are 'er drugs — and she just annihilates ... *reality* ... in the process. (*Beat.*) Makes life easier, I s'pose. (*Beat. He has a long drag on his cigarette.*) Gave her some advice, but.

Henry What?

Trevor Alec, the Americano. That guy we saw at *Who's Afraid of Virginia Woolf?* Sugar daddy. She 'as to dump 'im.

Henry Yeah.

Trevor She talked about 'im a lot.

Henry Did she?

Trevor She was drunk. Don't think many people know much about 'im. Actually, I think she was telling me so that I'd tell you. (*Beat. He smokes.*) He keeps her, yeah. We all know that. And they've ... you know ... (*indicates with his fingers*)

Henry (*to himself, very quietly*) Fuck ...

Trevor I thought you'd know. It's obvious, i'n't it?

(*Beat.*)

Henry (*resigned*) What did you do?

Trevor Huh?

Henry What did you do when you found out? What did you do?

Trevor I didn't do anything, mate. I'm not gonna do anything. What's to do? I seen 'im a few times, to be honest, I quite like the guy. Henry. There's nothing against fucking some sucker who gives you money, now, is there? That ain't illegal.

(*Beat.*)

Henry The whole thing ... it's all .... awful.

Trevor Leave it, she's working it out, I reckon. I told 'er she 'as to. Move on, you know? (*Beat.*) Have you ever 'eard of Sally Bowles?

Henry Yes.

Trevor Anne is just like 'er. (*Pause.*) And Sally Bowles was a bitch.

Henry I liked Sally Bowles.

Trevor God, mate, yeah. The perfect woman. (*Beat.*) Look, I um, 'ave to go in a minute.

Henry Yes.

Trevor You're all right.

Henry Is this what you do? Every night?

Trevor As long as it doesn't affect anyone else.

(*Beat.*)

Henry But it has. It does. Me.

(*Beat.*)

Trevor I've written a poem about this. I'm never guilty ... I never get into trouble.

(**Henry** grabs **Trevor**'s *hand.*)

(*jokingly*) Not 'ere mate. Decorum. Impressionable kids about!

(*Pause.*) How about coming out with me tomorra night? I mean it. I want to.

Henry OK, I will.

Trevor Great. Excellent. I'll call for you. (*Pause.*) Look, mate, I've got to go inside. Andromeda. (*Pause.*) It's nothin'.

Henry Yeah. I understand. I'll give you a call.

Trevor Let me know what you think of that poetry. I can't wait to hear your critical opinion, serious.

Henry I will.

Trevor See ya then.

Henry Bye.

> (**Trevor** *stands, then quickly bends and kisses* **Henry** *on the head.* **Henry** *tries to kiss him on the mouth.* **Trevor** *pulls back.*)

Trevor?

Trevor It's a sad world, i'n't it? So much crap.

> (*He exits. Beat.* **Henry** *sits and laughs dismissively to himself.*)

Henry Wanker.

> (*He looks out front. Music. Crossfade.*)

Scene 18

A pub, Neal's Yard. **Henry** *sits on his own. Long pause. Eventually,* **Anne** *appears, in a long coat, scarf, carrying a Harvey Nichols bag.*

Anne Henry?

> (*Pause.* **Henry** *looks around and sees her.*)

Henry Hi. I didn't know if you'd come.

Anne Usually, I go straight home, Henry. Usually I don't read messages given to me by the stage-door. I never took you for a stage-door Johnny.

Henry You never used to call me that, Henry. (*Beat.*) How're things?

Anne I'm all right. (*smiles*)

(*Pause.*)

Henry I saw a review.

Anne Which one?

Henry Don't remember. I saw your name ... thought I'd come to see it.

Anne Poor you.

Henry It's all right.

Anne (*sighs*) It's terrible. Not my thing and not yours either.

Henry I liked it. What can I get you?

Anne I'm not having anything. I can't stay.

Henry Not much of a pub, this.

(*Pause.*)

Anne I know you've been before, Henry. (*Beat.*) It's a bit hard to sneak out before curtain-call in that theatre. (*Beat.*) That was really silly. (*Beat.*) Not letting me know.

(*Beat.*)

Henry Are you OK?

Anne Stop asking me that. Why wouldn't I be?

Henry I worry ... everything. I miss you. I want to know why you didn't tell me you were in a new play. I want to know ... what's ... happened ...

(*Pause.*)

Anne I've got some film work.

Henry Oh. Anne! That's wonderful. Congratulations.

(*Pause. She looks away.*)

Anne When this has finished you won't see me on stage for a while, I hope. Or in London. (*Beat.*) It's been too cold for me here lately.

Henry This is what you've wanted for ages.

Anne Yes.

Henry I suppose Alec's pleased.

Anne Why do you bring him up?

(*He makes no answer.*)

I know that you know that I've dumped him.

Henry What do you mean?

Anne What do I mean? What do you mean, asking me? Don't ask me questions.

(*Beat.*)

Henry This is almost the West End, Anne. You're almost acting in the West End.

Anne I don't give a brass razoo about that.

(*Pause.*)

Henry I didn't know what to think ... I thought ... I knew it was coming. Shit. He's a funny guy, Trevor.

(*Beat.* **Anne** *looks upwards.*)

Anne Really, Frappy, I haven't seen Trevor for a long time.

Henry I'm worried. Scared. You don't know all about him. (*rubs his temple*) If you only knew what was going on up here.

Anne It's in France. (*Pause.*) I'm going away for a good while. (*Pause.*) Yes. I'm going to France. The pay's good. Better than ever. (*Pause.*) I'm going to France! Maybe I'll meet a Frenchman and turn into the next ... (*She stops.*) Maybe not. (*Beat.*) I feel calm. Everything is just so. (*Beat.*) Trevor, Frappy, is stupid. Not stupid, pointless. Yes. One of those pointless ... (*searching for the word; angry*) ... pervs. But, he can ... at least he can ... articulate, can't he? He can talk. Sense, amazingly. (*Beat.*) Poor Henry.

(*Beat.*)

Henry I was so jealous. He was mine. You were mine.

Anne That was selfish of you.

Henry I felt betrayed. Still do. (*looks away*)

Anne No one betrayed you. I never lied. (*Pause.*) Don't come at me with all this crap now. It's too *late*. Who cares now?

> (*Long, long pause. She looks at him. She looks away. Eventually, he faces her.*)

Henry What's your part?

Anne It's a tiny, weeny, minuscule thing.

Henry A love interest?

Anne Sort of. It's a bit hard to explain. Very Merchant Ivory!

> (*Pause.*)

Henry Gordon's for lunch tomorrow?

Anne I can't.

Henry No, I can't, either.

Anne You see him, right? Trevor.

Henry (*nods*) Whenever I can.

Anne Really?

> (**Henry** *nods.*)

Send him my love, then.

Henry Maybe. Yes. (*Pause.*) I think we might move in together.

Anne (*surprised*) What?

Henry I think I might ask him to move in with me.

Anne Why?

Henry I ... I ... like him. I think.

Anne Do you really?

Henry Yes. (*Beat.*) I think.

Anne I don't know why.

Henry I don't either.

Anne Can you trust him?

Henry It's not the same for him.

> (*Pause.*)

Anne *You're* stupid. I can't believe you, saying that. "It's not

103

the same for him" ... Trust is trust. Someone like ... *that* ... he's ... You're dumb.

Henry I've never denied it. We all are.

(*Beat.*)

Anne (*blasé*) He was a bit of a lecher.

(*Long pause. He is not looking at her.*)

I want to carefully turn your head, so that you're looking into my eyes. Stare into my face, Frappy. (*Beat.*) You've got such gorgeous hair, I've always loved it. (*Beat.*) I won't miss London. Fresh fields!

Henry (*turns to her*) Shall I wish you good luck?

Anne If you want to.

(*They look at each other. Music. Crossfade.*)

Scene 19

Outside **Trevor**'s *flat. Late at night.* **Trevor** *sits on the steps to the main entrance. He has been drinking and has a whisky bottle.* **Henry** *walks up.*

Henry (*to a cat*) Pppsstt, you little fucker!

(*Pause.*)

Trevor Hey, Hen.

Henry Trevor! What are you doing outside? It's freezing.

(*He sits down next to him.*)

Trevor (*offers the bottle*) Have a drink?

Henry Thanks, I will.

Trevor A fag?

Henry Yeah, that too. (*Beat.*) Are you all right?

(**Trevor** *nods. Beat.*)

I went to see Anne.

Trevor Did you? Get it sorted?

Henry I think.

Trevor I hope so. (*Beat.*) I reckon our troubles are just beginning, mate.

(*Beat.*)

Henry I'm here to tell you something. Anne's gone away. Martin's moving out of the flat. He's going to live with Sally, or whatever her name is.

Trevor Really?

Henry Yeah.

Trevor He's doing the right thing.

Henry Is he?

Trevor Oh, yeah. Shouldn't stay in a dump like that for too long.

Henry So you do think it's a dump?

Trevor It's the worst, mate, your place is the worst.

(*Pause.* **Henry** *laughs.*)

Bad for someone like that guy.

(*Pause.*)

Henry (*shyly*) I'll be looking for someone ... When does your lease expire?

Trevor Dunno, mate.

Henry Would you consider ... leaving here?

Trevor Just right for me 'ere, wordsmith. (*Beat.*) I could check, though, think about it ... we could ...

(*He looks away.*)

Henry I thought you'd be out tonight.

Trevor No, not tonight.

Henry I've borrowed a friend's car. Thought I'd check to see if you were in.

Trevor I'm in.

(*Pause.*)

Henry I haven't heard any of your poems for a while.

Trevor I gave you that one ...

Henry Oh, yeah. Sorry. I haven't read it yet.

Trevor Paahh! I 'aven't written anythin' for a long time. Too busy. It's bullshit.

> (**Caroline** *enters.*)

Caroline Well, hello boys.

Henry Hello, Caroline.

Caroline How are you both?

Henry All right. Thanks.

Caroline (*to* **Trevor**) Not out tonight?

> (*No answer.*)

Are you waiting for something? Someone?

Henry Just talking.

Caroline It's cold.

Henry Yeah.

> (*Beat.*)

Caroline (*to* **Trevor**) You're quiet. (*Pause.*) Isn't he quiet? I've never heard anything like it. Hello? (*Pause.*) Are you mute? Did a trick get your tongue?

Henry Caroline ...

Caroline (*over this*) What have you done to him?

> (*Pause. She looks at* **Trevor**.)

Trevor Where've you been?

Caroline That's more like it. Out. With friends. Somewhere you've never been.

> (*Beat.* **Trevor** *looks away.* **Caroline** *is uncomfortable.*)

(*to* **Henry**) I can't work it out, what you see in him.

Henry What do you mean?

Caroline Nothing.

Henry No, what do you mean?

(**Caroline** *looks hard at* **Trevor**.)

Caroline Are you all right? Trevor? (*Beat.*) Trevor?

(*Pause. He says nothing. She makes her way upstairs.*)

Apart from me, but I don't count, you're the only person I've ever known who's put up with him for more than six months.

Trevor (*quietly, looking at* **Henry**) It's getting on to a year now, i'n't it, mate?

Henry Yeah, almost a year.

(*Beat.* **Trevor** *looks away.*)

Caroline Most people I know ... (*tails off*)

Henry Yes?

(*Pause.*)

Caroline Most people I know just end up telling him to fuck off. Well, goodnight.

(*She exits. Long pause.* **Henry** *smokes, puts his cigarette out and has a swig of whisky.*)

Trevor (*quietly*) I had a bad day today.

(*Pause.*)

Henry Why?

Trevor I went to give blood.

Henry Oh ... really?

Trevor I 'aven't given blood for ages. I always used to when I was a bit younger. Mum used to do it as well. She'd take me to the blood bank in Dorchester and we'd do it together. I remember once I said I'd eaten but I 'adn't and when I came out afterwards I was on cloud five 'undred and fifty-nine. I 'aven't been as 'igh since.

(**Henry** *laughs. Pause.*)

Henry I haven't given blood.

Trevor You'd be OK, mate. (*Pause; uncertain*) I think you would. (*Beat.*) You should. (*Beat.*) It's something really worthwhile.

Henry So did ... you give blood today?

> (**Trevor** *looks at* **Henry** *long and hard. His expression is pained, innocent.*)

Trevor (*stammers*) I ... I couldn't ...

Henry What do you mean?

Trevor I couldn't, mate. They wouldn't let me. Well, it's not that they wouldn't let me. But I couldn't fill out the form.

> (*Beat.*)

Henry Trevor — (*stops*)

Trevor (*backs away*) I couldn't fill it out, you know? Not without lyin'. And I couldn't lie, this time, I just couldn't.

Henry Trevor ...

Trevor I'm a risk. I couldn't give blood. I'm a risk ...

> (*He shakes his head and begins to cry. He knocks over the whisky bottle and begins to grope for it, but the tears pour from his eyes and he loses his sight.* **Henry** *takes him in his arms.*)

(*sobbing*) I couldn't give blood ... I couldn't give blood ....

Henry Oh, Trevor ...

Trevor ... they wouldn't let me give blood ...

Henry Shhhhh. Ssshhh. Oh, Trevor ... ssshhhhh ...

> (**Henry** *holds* **Trevor** *tight and rocks him. Music. Crossfade.*)

Scene 20

Trevor's *flat.* **Henry** *sits on his own, writing in his diary. Long pause.* **Trevor** *enters.*

Trevor Look at you, writin' away. You're like me, I'm like that: head down, don't let anyone disturb me, get everythin' on paper, then I re-work it. Saw a Burroughs film once, apparently you shouldn't do that, not if you've got real talent, that's censorin' yourself.

(*Pause.* **Henry** *doesn't look up.*)

What's that?

Henry What?

Trevor That.

Henry It's a letter.

Trevor Who from?

Henry Anne.

Trevor In France?

Henry Yeah.

Trevor She's still there.

Henry Yes.

Trevor You 'aven't opened it.

Henry No, I will, later.

Trevor That's bad luck, that is. Rotten omen if you leave it for too long. I wonder what she's up to? France. Wow. I wonder when the film'll be out.

Henry I read that it might not get a release here.

Trevor Oh. Shame. We'll 'ave to go and see it over there, eh? Maybe not. Whatcha think of this hair?

Henry It looks fine.

Trevor Shall I cut it a bit more? The scissors are blunt, but. Do you wanna cup of tea?

Henry (*smiling*) No.

      (**Trevor** *exits, smiling.* **Caroline** *knocks on the door and enters.*)

Caroline Hello ...?

Henry Come in.

Caroline Oh, hello.

Henry Hello.

Caroline I've only come to —

Trevor (*off*) Who's that?

Caroline Caroline.

(**Trevor** *bounds in.*)

Trevor Caroline! Caz! You're here to get what was it?

Caroline My book.

Trevor Yeah, got it. While you're 'ere, I've got some news. I've just bought a cappuccino maker and Henry's bought a new sooper-dooper video machine.

Caroline So?

Trevor I'm getting out *Helter Skelter* tonight. And *Victor/Victoria* tomorrow night.

Caroline I haven't seen either one of those.

Trevor Seen both, ten times apiece.

Caroline There's something different about you.

Trevor Is there? No, there isn't. I'm the same, same old me. (*Pause.*) Hey, Caroline, I'm moving to Clapham.

Caroline Clapham?

Trevor Yep, Clapham, South London.

Caroline Trevor?

Trevor It's all arranged.

Caroline What are you talking about?

Trevor I'm moving.

Caroline You're kidding ...

Trevor Nup! Zippidy-doo-dah! I'm off!

Caroline What about your lease?

Trevor Fuck 'im.

Caroline But you can't just ... leave.

Trevor Why not?

Caroline There are ... commitments ... aren't there? ... here ...

Trevor Who to? To whom? I'm getting out! My new poem is called "Paddington Snare".

Caroline The lease ...

Trevor Come on! Sod it! I given him enough capital over the past few years, I'm out of 'ere! We're both out of 'ere!

Caroline Are you two ...? (*indicates with her hands*)

Henry (*looking up*) Yes, Caroline, he's moving in with me.

Caroline It won't last.

> (*Beat. They all look at each other. Tension.* **Trevor** *bursts out laughing.* **Henry** *laughs too.*)

Trevor Nothing does, Caroline! Whatever lasts?

Caroline When are you going?

Trevor Sunday. (*Beat.*) Or the following one.

Caroline Stars. I can't believe it.

Trevor Getting away! You should try it.

Caroline I give it a week.

Trevor You'll miss me, won't you?

Caroline No, Trevor, I won't.

Trevor Liar.

> (*Music.* **Trevor** *smiles as* **Caroline** *stares.* **Henry** *looks up from his diary as the lights fade around him. He stares out front. Music very loud.*)
> (*Blackout.*)

The End.